The Humanist Approach to Happiness:

Practical Wisdom

To Linda -
Be Happy - Don't worry.

Jen Harrod
1-16-11

The Humanist Approach to Happiness:

Practical Wisdom

by

Jennifer S. Hancock

Published 2010
Printed by CreateSpace in the United States of America

Text copyright 2009 by Jennifer S. Hancock

ISBN: 1453651705
EAN-13: 9781453651704

http://www.jen-hancock.com

I want to thank my mother and father for inspiring me all these years. My husband for being so amazing and generous by providing me with the time I needed to write this book. To the Humanists of Florida Association for giving me the opportunity to not only work with so many amazing people but for also giving me the opportunity to work as a professional Humanist. And finally I want to thank everyone who has influenced me, been my friend, or provided food for thought throughout my life.

The Humanist Approach to Happiness

by Jennifer S. Hancock

Table of Contents

The Pursuit of Happiness

"There is no duty we so underrate as the duty of being happy. By being happy we sow anonymous benefits upon the world."

- Robert Louis Stevenson

I was raised as a Humanist, though we didn't use the term. My parents taught me to be responsible, compassionate, and ethical. I was taught that my actions have consequences, that happiness can be found, and that ultimately what is important is our relationships to other people.

When I finally realized that my personal piecemeal philosophy had a name, I found myself in a community of like-minded individuals dedicated to making the world a better place. I eventually found work within this movement, serving as the executive director for a state association of Humanists in Florida. Through that work I was privileged to get to know some amazing people and was able to explore my understanding of the philosophy and how it can be applied to daily life.

I decided to write this book after a troubling conversation with my neighbor's teenage daughter. She had no idea how to live her life so that she would be happy, though it was clear she desperately wanted to be. Specifically it was her lack of understanding about what constitutes a romantic relationship that made me want to write this book. When she was 15 years old she told me that she was upset her boyfriend hadn't called her in a few weeks. Upon questioning, he turned out to be a boy she had had sex with, but never actually dated. She was pretty stunned when I told her that this boy wasn't her boyfriend and that he was probably never going to call her. The choices she was making about her relationships, education, and other aspects of her life were not well informed. Worse, she was oblivious to the fact that her actions had consequences that were negatively impacting her happiness.

What Is Happiness?

"Happiness and the creative realization of human needs and desires, individually and in shared enjoyment, are continuous themes of humanism."

– Humanist Manifesto II

Happiness is an emotional state and therefore a bit vague in its definition. When Humanists talk about happiness, we aren't just talking about the pursuit of idle pleasures. We are talking about a deep sense of well-being. This is one of those things that you must feel in order to understand, and which most people want but have no idea how to attain.

Responsibility Is Not a 4-letter Word

> "People think responsibility is hard to bear. It's not. I think that sometimes it is the absence of responsibility that is harder to bear."
>
> — Henry Kissinger

One key to being happy is contained in this utilitarian description of happiness: People are happy when they are "in control," that is, when they feel competent to satisfy their needs and reach their goals. There can be no happiness without personal control. And this is why Humanists place such a strong emphasis on personal responsibility.

People often treat *responsibility* as if it is a bad word, something we should avoid if we want to be happy. Just the opposite is true. Freedom, and therefore happiness, can only be achieved through responsibility. When you accept responsibility for your life, you gain control over it in a way that is unparalleled. No longer a victim of fate, you can do something to improve your life and the lives of those around you.

Your Moral Compass

> "Happiness comes when your work and words are of benefit to yourself and others."
>
> — The Buddha

Being responsible will only lead to happiness if it is guided by compassion. Compassion is the most important value you can have. Given how important compassion is to human happiness, it comes as no surprise to find that compassion is the basis for most ethical and moral codes on the planet.

There are two aspects of compassion that make it such an important ingredient to personal happiness. The first is that compassion is motivated by love—and that is a wonderful emotion to feel. Another reason to be compassionate is that it is impossible to be a good person without being a compassionate person. And it really is hard to feel good about yourself if you aren't a good person.

Expanding Our Morality

Being good is all about acting in an ethical and compassionate way with others. We know not to harm members of our family because we understand that they will hurt, like we will. As we grow in our learning, we find that we expand our compassion from our immediate family to our tribe, and from the tribe to increasingly wider groups of "others."

For Humanists this expansion of whom we consider compassionately and therefore treat ethically includes all human beings on the planet and not just a subset. This is the main reason why we call ourselves Humanists. We cannot transcend societal problems such as racism, genderism, and theocratic disputes without transcending the tribalism that is at the root of those views. We can only transcend those biased views with compassion.

Humanism

> "People spend a lifetime searching for happiness; looking for peace. They chase idle dreams, addictions, religions, even other people, hoping to fill the emptiness that plagues them. The irony is the only place they ever needed to search was within."
>
> *- Ramona Anderson*

The Humanist approach to happiness is simple:
- Happiness can only be achieved through freedom.
- Freedom can only be achieved through responsibility.
- And responsibility is most effective at contributing to happiness when it is in the service of compassion.

Freedom, responsibility, and compassion: these are the keys to the Humanist approach to happiness.

Using This Book

> "The purpose of morality is to teach you, not to suffer and die, but to enjoy yourself and live."
>
> *-Ayn Rand*

This book explores the many ways in which the Humanist approach to happiness can be implemented in our daily lives. By tackling the big and the small problems we each encounter throughout our lives, from taking care of our bodies to dealing with relationships and grief, the Humanist approach to happiness is laid out in its practical form.

The key to this approach is to take control over your destiny by taking responsibility for your actions and choosing to act in such a way that you maximize your happiness and the happiness of others.

The Rule of Threes

"Without freedom of thought, there can be no such thing as wisdom."

- Cato

Humanists consider rational thinking essential to good moral reasoning. Because rational thinking is so important, Humanists engage in a method of thinking called "Freethought." Freethinking is best thought of as an attempt to free your reasoning of self-or society-imposed limitations. It is hard to do because it requires a lot of self-discipline to realize when you are limiting your thinking and to actively consider alternatives. To help make sure I am considering alternatives in my thinking, I developed what I call the rule of threes.

The Rule of Threes Explained

"Three Rules of Work: Out of clutter find simplicity; from discord find harmony; in the middle of difficulty lies opportunity."

- Albert Einstein

The rule of threes is simple. Whenever you find yourself in a situation where you are trying to make a decision, make sure you consider at least three options. If you think you only have two options, you are missing something. If you force yourself to consider at least three options, you will generally ensure that you have covered your bases thoroughly.

I can't express how important it is to always remember the rule of threes. The nice thing about this rule is that it is simple. It is easy to remember three things, so it simplifies your thinking. It also has the ability to expand your thinking, because we all have a tendency to think in terms of black and white and remembering to consider the grays is always a good idea.

You can apply this rule in every aspect of your life. Consider what you are going to eat for dinner. Should you go out to eat? Cook In? How about having something delivered? There are at least three options. What are you going to do tonight? Watch a movie? Play a game? Read a book? There it is again, at least three options. This is not to imply that there might not be more options, but if you can't come up with at least three, you're not trying.

There is great comic book series written by Neil Gaiman titled *Sandman*. One of the stories involved a playwright. In his dream, he had climbed to the top of a hill. He is hanging on for dear life. He thinks he has only two choices: hang on for dear life, or let go and fall to his death. The Sandman points out that there was a third option: in your dreams, sometimes when you let go, you fly.

Putting It into Practice

> *"All persons ought to endeavor to follow what is right, and not what is established."*
>
> *-Aristotle*

The power of this rule comes when you are under stress. It is often when we feel most stuck that we forget to consider all our options. This is because problems are often posed to us as either/or scenarios. Whenever someone tries to convince you that there are only two options: either we do "A" or we do "B," the easy third option is the possibility that you could do both "A" and "B." You usually can do neither as a viable third option. Then there is the possibility that there is an option "C" that wasn't presented. I have yet to come across a situation where there are only two choices available. If you are in a situation where someone poses a problem to you in this way, the person is likely either trying to manipulate you or is not thinking clearly.

A perfect example of this is the debate about the death penalty. Most often, this is presented as either kill them or let them go. The reality is that when we have a person convicted of murder, there are many possible punishments. We could kill them, put them in prison for twenty years, put them in prison for life, or let them go with a fine. The question of what we do with people convicted of murder is not simply a kill-them-or-let-them-go situation. We have many options to choose from, but unless we actually discuss them, we will never be able to create a reasonable public policy on this issue.

Freethought in Action

"It is not enough to have a good mind, the main thing is to use it well."

- Rene Descartes

To be happy, you need to take responsibility for your actions, which requires that you think clearly and critically about all your options before making a decision. Don't constrain your thinking. Take it upon yourself to think up at least three or more solutions to any given problem. Not only will people around you think you are a genius; you will also find that you are able to think yourself out of most difficult situations. Being able to think yourself free of problems is a great way to gain control over your life and to not be swayed by people who wish you harm.

A word of warning: once you begin to practice Freethought, you will wonder how you ever made reasonable decisions before. You will learn how easy it is to make better decisions that more positively impact your life and therefore your happiness simply by thinking before you act. This newfound knowledge of the tangible benefits of Freethought will probably make you less patient with those who do not practice the technique. Just remember, a little compassion goes a long way.

The True Holy Trinity

"One ought to seek out virtue for its own sake, without
being influenced by fear or hope, or by any external
influence. Moreover, in that does happiness consist."
- Diogenes Laertius, Zeno

Humanism is first and foremost a philosophy about morality. It is the study of what it means to be a good human being. For me, there are three traits I consider mandatory for a person to be good. I call these three traits the true holy trinity. A good person is compassionate, ethical, and responsible. These are the things that matter the most.

Why Are These Traits So Important?

"Happiness is not a matter of events; it depends upon the
tides of the mind."

- Alice Meynell

There is a good reason why being ethical, compassionate, and responsible make you a good person. If a person is missing just one of these traits, they can't be trusted. For instance, if a person is ethical and compassionate, but not responsible, you can't trust them to do what they say they will. If they are compassionate and responsible but not ethical you can't trust what they say. If they are ethical and responsible but not compassionate, they can be trusted to keep their word but may be willing to cause harm to others to get what they want. All three traits are necessary to be a good person. Everything else is just window dressing.

Morality and Religion

Many people think it takes religion to be a good person. For me, it doesn't matter how you get there, only that you learn these three character traits and exemplify them in your life. In my experience there is no belief system that corners the market on these traits. There are wonderful Christians and there are some not so wonderful Christians. There are also wonderful atheists and some not so wonderful atheists. As my father always says, no group corners the market on stupidity.

Don't make assumptions about a person's moral or ethical character based on what their belief system is. Respect everyone by treating each person as an individual. Judge people based on their behavior and treat them accordingly. If you discriminate against people because of their faith, you will miss out on knowing some truly wonderful people. It is also wise to be cautious about trusting people just because they share your faith. You may end up being taken for a ride by an unscrupulous person.

True Traits of Virtue

> *"Waste no more time arguing about what a good man should be. Be one."*
>
> *- Marcus Aurelius*

Ethical

The word *ethical*, in this context, refers to a group of traits. If someone is ethical, they are honest, principled, fair, and decent. An ethical person has a sense of justice and knows the difference between right and wrong. They do not like to see other people taken advantage of or treated unfairly. Being ethical is essential to the holy trinity of goodness because without it, you will harm others. If you lie, cheat, steal, or treat people unfairly, the result is the same: someone is inevitably hurt, and that person is usually you.

Compassionate

Compassion is the most important attribute of this true holy trinity. It trumps the other two because it acts as a moral compass. It is impossible to be a good person without also being a compassionate person. A compassionate person wants to help others and cause no harm. Compassionate people are by nature kind, caring, sympathetic, empathetic, and considerate of others.

To be compassionate, you need to see other people as full human beings. Once you understand that other people feel love, pain, and sorrow exactly like you do, you begin to understand how important it is for you to become responsible for the impact your behavior has on others.

For a compassionate person, *good* is defined as helping people and *bad* is defined as hurting people. For a person who lacks compassion, good and bad are not defined this way and such a person may be willing to harm others to achieve their goals. An example of this is someone who values wealth over everything else. What does it matter if a person is honest and responsible if he or she doesn't care who gets hurt in pursuit of profits?

A person who lacks compassion is capable of astonishing horrors. Someone who lacks compassion can easily rationalize genocide or torture because what he or she values isn't human welfare. Hitler was such a person. He was by all accounts an honest and responsible person, but he was also willing to harm and kill large numbers of people to attain what he considered to be a "greater good." Whenever someone talks of a "greater good" or a "higher law," know that you are dealing with someone who is lacking compassion, and who is therefore a very dangerous person. Wise people steer clear of these sorts.

Responsible

Being responsible is part of the true holy trinity of goodness because it is not enough to be honest and fair. It is not enough to care and not wish to cause harm. Unless we take responsibility for our actions and the impact our actions have on others, we cannot hope to behave in a way that is good. A responsible person is conscientious, accountable, dependable and trustworthy. You can rely on a responsible person.

While ethics and compassion are both about how you think, being responsible is about how you actually act. It is not enough to want to do good. You can only be a good person by actually doing good. A person who is not responsible can be the nicest, most well-meaning person in the world, but what good does it do to be honest and compassionate if you do not put these fine attributes into action? It really isn't that hard to be a good person. A person who isn't, isn't trying.

Dealing with the Not So Good

> "To be nobody but yourself in a world which is working night and day to make you like everybody else means to fight the hardest battle any human being can fight and never stop fighting."
>
>   -e.e. cummings

I have a simple rule. I only make friends with people who are ethical, compassionate, and responsible. If a person is missing one of these traits, I treat them with respect as far as they earn it but do not become a close personal friend with them. As a result, I have an excellent group of friends. Unfortunately, because I live in the real world, I can't only interact with people I deem to be good. Sometimes, I am forced to deal with people who are not so good. It is important to have a strategy for dealing with these not-so-good people so that you can minimize the negative impact these people can have on your life.

While it might be obvious that you should watch out for people who aren't ethical, responsible, or compassionate, it is not so obvious to watch out for people who shine in one of these areas, but are lacking in the rest. They must have all three traits to qualify as a good person. Here are few particularly dangerous types of people that you should watch out for, and why.

Liar, Liar, Pants on Fire

If someone claims to be honest but then acts in a dishonest way, you would be an idiot to trust them. Until you know if you can trust someone's word, pay attention to what they do to confirm their honesty. If you have confirmed that you have been lied to, treat everything that person says with a grain of salt. Many people who lie do so pathologically, which means they lie about everything, including inconsequential things. As a rule of thumb, the more inconsequential and easily found out the lie is, the more likely the person is pathological about their lying.

It is best to have as little to do with liars as possible. Liars make life unnecessarily more complicated than it needs to be. If you can't avoid interacting with them because you work with them or they are in your family, the best you can do is work around them.

Your basic strategy for dealing with a liar is to protect yourself from any negative consequences that might result from their lies. If the consequences of a lie are important, get independent verification or enlist other people to help. If it is inconsequential, don't waste your time. Don't bother confronting a liar about their lies either. A liar will deny it, promise not to do it again, and/or blame someone else. You should assume that any and all statements a liar makes when caught in a lie are also lies.

Honesty Mavens

If you meet someone who is brutally honest about their past, and sometimes their present, you have met an honesty maven. Honesty mavens will tell you the wrongs committed in their pasts, the demons that are hiding in their closets, and how important they feel it is to be honest about their current problems. At first glance, it looks like the honesty maven is taking responsibility for his or her actions. However, approach any honesty maven with extreme caution.

Everyone recognizes honesty as being an essential component to being a good person, so the honesty maven attempts to overwhelm you with honesty as a way to distract you from his or her irresponsible behavior and/or lack of compassion. A mistake compassionate people make is in forgiving honesty mavens for past transgressions. Be warned: unless a person has changed their behavior and become responsible, you can't trust them.

For Example

If a person admits to having a drinking problem, but doesn't change their behavior and stop drinking, what has changed? Nothing. While the first step to overcoming an addiction is to admit to having a problem, it is only the first step. You need to apologize to others for the harm you have caused (an exercise in compassion), and then stop drinking (an exercise in responsibility). To only admit to having a problem isn't enough.

True Evil

While there are people who fail to be truly good, that doesn't necessarily make them evil. Most people want to be good. The only people I classify as evil are those who intentionally cause harm, especially if it is on a massive scale.

If an evil person is run of the mill, then the scope of the harm caused is limited. Evil people, if allowed to be in positions of power, are capable of major earth-shattering harm. Think Hitler, think Saddam Hussein, think Kim Jung Il, think Nero. These are evil people. Each may have thought that the evil they were performing was in service to a greater good (except for Nero), but all were unrepentantly responsible for the killing, torture, and misery of entire countries. Good people have a moral responsibility to not allow such people to become leaders. The problem is that the most evil of people still have their supporters. Don't be one of them.

The big problem is how to tell when a leader is truly evil. Truly evil people are simply not compassionate. If they tolerate human rights violations, or try to justify them, they are evil. If they develop a cult of personality around them, they are evil. If they don't tolerate dissent, they are evil. If they lie repeatedly, despite overwhelming evidence to the contrary, they are evil. If they continually demonize their opposition, they are evil.

You can also tell evil people by their followers. Are their followers mean? Do they demonize people or advocate ill treatment of anyone considered "other"? Do their followers make jokes in poor taste that only bigots would find funny? If so, the politician they are supporting is probably evil. Evil leaders attract ignorant and mean-spirited followers.

When it comes to politics, the stakes really are high. Make sure you don't support someone who is evil. Your best defense against true evil is to make sure you know what all sides of the political spectrum are saying and do your own research to find out who is actually telling the truth. This means you need to fact check both sides. When in doubt, always err on the side of compassion.

Suicidal Tendencies

When someone routinely acts in a way that puts their health and their life in danger, it is best to consider them as having suicidal tendencies. These are folks that you should not become friends with. In fact, you should run for the hills because people with suicidal tendencies usually don't want to die alone.

How do you recognize people with suicidal tendencies? Suicidal people often do things that will directly endanger their health. I once knew a woman who despite having a broken back still insisted that she be allowed to go out jet skiing. At that moment I knew she was suicidal. She eventually cheated on her boyfriend, became a heroin addict, and died in police custody. I wasn't surprised. She seemed nice enough, but she routinely made bad decisions that put her and those who cared about her in danger.

Heavy drug use or other addiction is another way to tell. And yes, I know many addicts consider their addictions a disease. But before they got addicted, they made a choice, and that choice was to take an addictive, life-destroying drug. So, until and unless they break their addiction, you should consider them suicidal and avoid them.

If someone keeps making bad decisions, there is something wrong with them. I have had two friends commit suicide and another attempt it, and this is in addition to the woman I described above. Not one of them ever talked about suicide or about killing themselves. Instead for years they all engaged in risky behavior. These behaviors included drug use, sex with total strangers, going off trail when hiking in the desert, and, in one case, obsessive cigarette smoking and caffeine use. Whenever you find yourself wondering why a friend is behaving badly and doing things that are clearly risky, you seriously need to consider the possibility that your friend simply doesn't care whether they live or die.

Unfortunately, I have no good advice on how to deal with people who have a death wish. The common information on suicide prevention doesn't seem applicable. I do know that I wish I had known how to recognize the signs that indicated my friends were in fact suicidal. Suicide prevention websites will tell you to take your suspicion that someone is suicidal seriously. I agree. Trying to get help for a friend who is suicidal is always a good idea. But you also need to be cognizant of your own safety if that help is refused. When you hang out with people who do risky things, you put your own life at risk as well.

As callous as it seems, my advice is actually to avoid suicidal people as much as possible and don't get too emotionally attached. The likelihood is that they will eventually succeed in killing themselves and you don't want to die as part of their collateral damage when that happens.

On Being a Good Person

> *"Action may not always bring happiness; but there is no happiness without action."*
> *- Benjamin Disraeli*

Most people want to be good, so the motivation to be good is there. It is not unusual, however, for people to fall short of this ideal. How can you assure yourself that you are meeting your own high standards for good behavior? The answer is to be an ethical, compassionate, and responsible person. Do not allow even one of these traits to take a back seat to expediency. You must be all three of these things all the time. Don't worry; being good is easier than it sounds.

The driving emotion that will help you want to be good is your compassion. You must care about what happens to yourself and to the people around you. Without compassion you won't care enough to do the right thing. After that, your next task is to be responsible. Think before you act. How are your actions going to impact your life and the lives of those around you? Making sure your behavior is ethical, and honest is the best way to make sure that impact is good.

On the Necessity of Being Polite

> *"If you want to slide through life, try being nice."*
> *- Christopher Shaw*

Part of being a nice person is being polite. There are very few reasons to justify rudeness. Be nice to everyone you meet. Your niceness will be returned. Plus, you never know if someone was having a bad day, and being nice might help turn their day around.

This is especially important when dealing with the various service personnel you encounter every day. It is always amazes me how many people take their frustrations out on sales clerks, waiters, postal workers, toll booth workers, and others, simply because they had to wait a little longer than they wanted to.

Don't underestimate how important being nice is. When you are nice you make real human connections with other real people. And that alone is worth the effort, especially since being nice doesn't cost you anything. When you think about trying to be nice to the people serving you, you replace anger with compassion and frustration with happiness.

Do not equate being polite with showing respect. You can and should be polite to everyone, including and especially people you don't respect. Being polite greases the wheels of interpersonal relations and helps avoid unnecessary conflict.

If you encounter a situation where being nice puts you in a position where you will be hurt, either emotionally or physically, your obligation to be polite is temporarily absolved. This doesn't happen very often, but when it does, you can rationalize your impolite behavior as necessary to get out of a bad situation.

For Example

If someone is physically threatening you, calling attention to the dangerous behavior in public, while it might not be in good taste, may just save your life. For women especially, there are men who will try to use your niceness to your disadvantage. They trust that you will not slap them, walk away, or scream at them in public. My advice is to follow your instincts. I have only slapped one person in my life and I didn't think about it before hand. It just happened. The other men who were present all said I did the right thing. I have also ditched a man in the middle of a date, and I am absolutely convinced I did the right thing. If I had known then what I know now, I would have ditched two other individuals who both put me in very dangerous situations because I was being too polite to protect myself. Be nice, but always put safety first.

Human Morality

> *"A good world needs knowledge, kindliness, and courage."*
> - Bertrand Russell

Humanist morality is very simple: If it helps, it is good; if it harms, it is bad. If your actions will do both, try to maximize the good and minimize the bad. This is why human compassion defines what it means to be truly good.

Being ethical, compassionate, and responsible are the traits of the true holy trinity. Cultivate these traits in yourself and look for these traits in others. If someone is missing one of these traits, be afraid. Be very afraid.

The World Doesn't Revolve Around You!

*"The happy man is not he who seems thus to others, but
who seems thus to himself."*

- Publilius Syrus

Humanism is an individualist philosophy. This individualism requires the recognition that every human being on the planet is in fact a real person worthy of basic levels of respect. While it is easy to talk a good talk about the dignity and worth of individual human beings, it turns out that actually treating real people with compassion and respect isn't all that easy. We all tend to get so wrapped up in our own issues that we forget other people have their own problems.

Now, listen to me closely. The sooner you get this, and I mean really get this, the easier your life will be and the more compassionate you will be. *The world doesn't revolve around you.* You are just one of the 6+ billion human beings on this planet we call Earth. Everyone one of your fellow human beings is as real as you are. They all have real issues, real struggles, real families, and real dreams, exactly like you.

Getting to Know You

*"Most people would rather be certain they're miserable,
than risk being happy."*

- Robert Anthony

Understanding that the world doesn't revolve around you will help you with your interpersonal relationships. People really do have their own problems that most likely have absolutely nothing to do with you. The real lesson here is not to take things personally.

If someone you meet on the street or in a shop is rude to you, it probably has nothing to do with you. There are myriad reasons why they might act that way. They could have cancer and be in a lot of pain. They could have recently lost a child. They could have recently broken up with someone, or lost a job. They could have a hormone imbalance, be mentally ill, or just plain ornery from a life of hardship. You don't know because you don't know them and what is motivating them at that particular moment. To assume someone is being rude to you because they don't like you is egotistical. Unless you have done something to make them mad at you, their behavior probably has nothing to do with you.

For Example

When I was in high school, one of the girls in my class took an immediate dislike to me and was really quite mean. I had no idea why this complete stranger didn't like me, so I did my best to avoid her. I eventually found out that way back in elementary school I had apparently insulted her and she had held a grudge against me into high school. This was a complete shock to me because I didn't know her in elementary school, as we went to different schools.

Here is apparently what happened. When I was in elementary school, I would often play with the middle school band (which my music teacher also taught). This girl had come to one of the middle school band performances and had approached me to find out how I had gotten into the middle school band. At the time I was really very shy and probably stared at her in silence (my standard response to a stranger at the time). She took my silence as a personal snub and when we got to high school the grudge she had nursed since elementary school blossomed.

Eventually we talked this out and became good friends. As a grade school student, she had not considered the possibility that my behavior had nothing to do with her. Once she realized that I hadn't snubbed her in grade school, that I was too shy to talk to a stranger, and that my attempts to ignore her in high school had nothing do to with the grade school incident of which I had no recollection, we were able to put it all behind us. I was even a bridesmaid at her wedding and we are still friends.

Know Thyself

> "No matter how dull, or how mean, or how wise a man is,
> he feels that happiness is his indisputable right."
> - Helen Keller

No one is immune to self-absorption. Not even me. I know that I am self-absorbed. My girlfriend from high school was right to be upset with me, just not for the right reasons. I hadn't purposely dissed her in grade school, but I hadn't bothered to pay any attention to her either.

The truth is, there are very few people I remember. There were over 600 students in my senior high school class. Out of those I probably had classes with less than 200 people. Of those, I was friendly with about 50 people. When I look at my high school yearbook I am at a complete loss. I hardly remember any of them. I'm not a shallow person, but unless they were important to me in some way, I don't remember them.

Let me say that again. Unless they were important to ME, I don't remember them. And this is what is at the heart of the problem. I mean, think about it: there are over 6 billion people on the planet. I can't be expected to know all of them.

Though you can't pay attention to everyone individually, it is important to remember that everyone one you meet is an individual with real dreams, desires, and day-to-day stresses, exactly like you. Recognizing other people as real helps you to be more compassionate with them. So, regardless of how other people act, try being nice. It doesn't cost you anything, and you may make their day, and yours, a little easier.

All in the Family

> "He is happiest, be he king or peasant, who finds peace in his home."
>
> *- Johann von Goethe*

These perception problems affect your family members as well. Even when you are close to someone, you can never really know what is going on inside someone else's head. They have myriad interactions and activities that they are dealing with on a daily basis that you may know nothing about. So, when it comes to family members, including brothers, sisters, mothers, and fathers, when they act strange, don't take it personally. Try to be compassionate and offer to support them as best you can. After all, if you don't, who will?

Transcendence

> "The world of those who are happy is different from the world of those who are not."
>
> *- Ludwig Wittgenstein*

Truly self-centered people are convinced that other people's actions are in direct response to their own. After all, they are the center of their own universe, so other people must be responding to them, right?

In reality, the people around you aren't behaving the way they do because of you. Most likely, they aren't even aware you exist. Because they have no idea you exist, it is ludicrous to think that they are doing things simply to annoy you. When you realize how hard it is for you to grasp this concept, you will finally understand that everyone else on the planet really is obsessed with his or her own life and not yours.

It isn't only self-centered people who do this. Almost everyone on the planet suffers from this perception problem to a greater or lesser extent, including me. When you recognize this tendency in yourself, you can make your life easier by recognizing your perception as flawed.

The Wisdom of Neo

> *"Happiness is not a destination. It is a method of life."*
> *- Burton Hills*

You will gain a greater benefit if you can recognize this perception difficulty in others. Why? Because when you stop thinking it is all about you, you start to understand why people are really behaving the way they do, and can respond accordingly. You will be like Neo in *The Matrix* when he finally gets that he is not experiencing reality, but is imagining it. It is only then that he can control what happens to him.

We cannot transcend our self-centered view of the world; the best we can do is to accept it and work around it. When you realize that the world doesn't actually revolve around you, you can choose to override your instinct that tells you it does. Knowing this will make you feel better immediately and could save your life.

Zen Driving

> *"Stay aware of your surroundings, don't let expectations distract you, and enjoy the ride."*
> *- Craig Clarke*

To better understand the problems of self-centered perception it is helpful to consider the effects of this mindset while driving. As amazing as it seems, most of the other drivers on the road are not actually aware of you. They may be vaguely aware of your car because they can see it, but they don't know you, how you think, what you ate for breakfast, where you are going, or what you plan to do next.

Not only can you increase your chances of not getting into an accident by understanding that the world doesn't revolve around you, this enhanced understanding of how other people think can help you avoid accidents. Once you know that the other drivers on the road think you see them and know what they are going to do next, you start to expect the unexpected.

Accident-free Driving

People who delude themselves into thinking that all the other drivers on the road are aware of them and know what they are planning to do next cause a lot of accidents. If a car you didn't know was on the road has ever cut you off, you have experienced this delusion in action.

Many drivers really believe that you can see them (even if you can't), that you know what they are planning to do next (even though you aren't aware of them), and that as a result, you will give them the right of way and not hit them. That is a lot of assumptions and results in a lot of accidents.

Obviously you need to apply this to your own behavior. Though you know what you are planning to do next, don't assume it is obvious to anyone else. It isn't unless you make it obvious. Since most drivers don't how to read your mind, clearly signal your intentions. That is what your signals are for.

The lesson here is to recognize that there are likely cars around you that you haven't seen yet, and that haven't seen you. Further, the drivers of these unseen cars are convinced that you have seen them and that you know what they are going to do next. Once you understand this you will have a better chance of avoiding accidents.

My Advice

Make it your responsibility to give others the right of way. Don't assume they see you and will avoid you. That is the mistake they are making. It doesn't matter who had the right of way if you are both in traction. Take the responsibility on yourself to avoid accidents whenever possible.

Practicing Humanism

> "If we are to have peace on earth, our loyalties . . . must
> transcend our race, our tribe, our class, and our nation;
> and this means we must develop a world perspective."
> - Martin Luther King Jr.

Understanding that each person in the world is a real person with real dreams, desires, and problems changes the way you view other people. This change is central to why the Humanist philosophy is called Humanism. Once you truly grasp the reality of other individuals, human rights are no longer a pithy slogan: they are a mandatory prerequisite for civilized living that must never be compromised.

To have meaning, respect for the dignity and worth of every individual in the abstract must be applied to how you treat the people you meet on a day-to-day basis. When you interact with someone, remember that they have their own problems and issues that have nothing to do with you. Treating everyone you meet ethically and compassionately not only eases interpersonal relationships, it will help you feel better about yourself and make you a better person.

What a Dork!

"The supreme happiness in life is the conviction that we are loved — loved for ourselves, or rather, loved in spite of ourselves."

- Victor Hugo

Freedom is the core of the Humanist approach to happiness. This freedom requires not only personal responsibility, but also compassion. To experience true happiness, we must apply both freedom and compassion to ourselves. This isn't always easy, as we are usually our own worst critics. What follows are some tips on how to be compassionate with yourself so that you can enjoy the freedom of being you.

What You Need to Know

"Nobody likes me, everyone hates me, I think I'll go eat some worms."

- *Children's Song*

You are a dork. As soon as you accept this, you will begin to be happy. How can I know you are a dork without meeting you? Because everyone on the planet is a dork. I am a dork, the president is a dork, your favorite rock star is a dork, nomads in the desert, everyone. And, in a strange twist of opposites,[1] the only people who are truly cool are those who are at one with their inner dork.

We all have dorkish tendencies. Our worst fear is that others will find us out. We spend an amazing amount of time and energy trying to suppress our true nature while pretending to be cool. As a result, we are not fully ourselves. We only allow ourselves to be truly dorky when we are alone, or with trusted friends. It is only in these unguarded moments that we are truly happy.

Almost everyone learns to be ashamed of their intrinsic dorkiness through childhood trauma/teasing. At some point we were our dorky little selves having fun and some uptight jerk made fun of us. We learn that being a dork is a bad thing. As we grow, we become more aware that others might disapprove of our uncensored enjoyment of life and so we suppress our dorky tendencies. The problem is that to be happy we need to be dorks. Being a dork means being free to be yourself.

---

[1] Twist of Opposites: We all know the maxim that for every action there is an equal and opposite reaction. The usual example of this is a rocket. By creating downward thrust, a rocket goes up, the opposite direction from the direction of the thrust. This concept actually applies to social activities as well. This is the twist of opposites. Thrust down, go up. Act like a dork, be cool.

I Think I'll Go Eat Some Worms

Everyone, and I mean everyone, has felt like everyone hates them at some point. This is why the children's song about eating worms is so popular and so funny. It speaks the truth.

We all have our ups and downs. Sometimes we think we are wonderful and darn it, people like us. Other times, we think we are so amazingly stupid that no one could possibly like us, and who told us we could [insert your favorite activity here] anyway, we must have been delusional. Everyone hates us and if they don't, they should. We might as well go eat some worms. That'll show them.

For most people, these fluxes between feeling great and feeling rotten are not too extreme or frequent. These fluxes are normal and, like every other emotion we feel, temporary. The important lesson is that when you are feeling this way, remember the song and don't take yourself too seriously.

The Good News

> *"Keep away from people who try to belittle your ambitions. Small people always do that, but the really great make you feel that you, too, can become great."*
>
> *- Mark Twain*

It turns out, being a dork means being an interesting and exceptional person. Truly cool people are at one with their inner dork. Take your favorite rock star for instance, or comedian, or actor/actress. One of the reasons they are the amazing performers that they are, is because they are not afraid to put themselves out there. Being afraid of what other people think will cause you to suppress your true dork nature and that means suppressing yourself.

There are a lot of mediocre people out there who are afraid that they will be exposed as dorks. Because they are afraid, they try to influence others to be afraid too, and for the most part they succeed. These are the bullies and jerks of the world; people who look down on open expressions of dorkiness so that they will not be found guilty by association.

You need not care what mediocre people think. You should only care what exceptional people think. Exceptional people are comfortable with who they are and they are at ease with other people expressing themselves freely. In fact, once you allow yourself to enjoy life without worrying about what others will think, you will find that you prefer the company of people who are also not afraid to be dorks.

Becoming One with Your Inner Dork

> *"The Humanist rarely loses the feeling of at-homeness in the universe."*
>
> A. Eustace Haydon

The best way to come to terms with your inner dorkiness is to do what you like to do, and don't worry about fitting in. You might not be tight with the "in crowd" but you will gather around you a circle of true friends who know who you are and like you anyway.

For Example

When I was in high school, I liked to eat lunch by myself. Not because I was unsocial, but because I value my quiet time. But it didn't matter what quiet corner of campus I found for myself, my friends gradually joined my quiet haven. By being myself, and not caring what other people thought, like-minded people were drawn to me. They understood who I was and liked me anyway. My friends will be the first to tell you that I am the world's biggest dork, and that is apparently one of the reasons why they like me.

Being at Peace

> *"Happiness results from a sense of mental and moral contentment with who we are, what we value, and how we invest our time and resources for purposes beyond ourselves."*
>
> - David Shi

The biggest benefit of allowing yourself to be the dork you truly are is that it doesn't take any extra energy. This is why truly cool people seem to be so calm. They don't spend any time trying to guess what others think they should be (which is an impossible task unless you are a mind reader), and they don't spend any energy trying to be something they are not (which is something that can only be sustained for short periods of time anyway).

When you meet people who are comfortable with whom they are, you will know immediately. They radiate a calm that cannot be faked. They are content with themselves and they don't put any pressure on you to be anything but who you are. If you suppress yourself they see through you immediately and may move on to someone more real and therefore more interesting. They are comfortable in crowds large and small. They can be seen eating at a restaurant by themselves. They don't care what others think, they simply are.

For Example

When I was younger, I played in a swing band. We had a guest conductor who worked with us periodically, named Jack Wheaton. He was Stan Kenton's protégé. What I remember most about him was how he behaved at one of our concerts. He was standing alone in the lobby of the hall prior to our performance. I had never seen anyone so comfortable being alone like that before. It made a strong impression on me, one I never forgot. He was the epitome of cool, calm, and collected.

On Becoming Cool

> "If practice makes perfect, and no one's perfect, then why practice?"
>
> - Billy Corgan

Being cool isn't about being wild and crazy. Being cool actually refers to an amused yet calm approach to life. To achieve this, you need to have a good sense of humor about yourself and engage in a certain amount of compassionate introspection. But don't worry; it is easier than it sounds.

How do you become cool? Like everything in life, practice makes perfect. People aren't born cool; they learn how to be cool. If you aren't used to applying humorous compassion to your life, you might feel a bit apprehensive. Don't worry about that. You don't have to feel comfortable at first. You just have to act as if you are. The more you practice, the easier it will become. Eventually, that inner voice of fear will subside and you will gain enough distance from it to find that voice humorous when it does sneak back into your consciousness.

A Simple Exercise

Try going to a nice restaurant by yourself. Most people would rather have elective dental surgery than do this, but if you want to learn to be cool, you need to confront your fear of being a dork head on. Going to a nice restaurant by yourself is a great way to overcome this fear. You can also practice being cool by going to the movies yourself, going to an amusement park alone, and any other activities that you wouldn't normally think of doing by yourself. The more you do things by yourself, the more comfortable you will become with yourself.

One of the main benefits of doing things only "dorks" do by themselves is that you don't have to have someone else's approval to enjoy yourself. Because you don't have to have someone else's approval, you will soon learn to enjoy the freedom that comes with being truly you. Once you experience this freedom, you will never want to relinquish it again. When you are okay with who you are when you are alone, you are much less likely to change who you are when you are with a group.

My Life as a Dork

One time when I was at Disneyland with some friends, we were waiting in line to get lunch when we met a woman by herself. She had taken her kids to the park and they had run off and left her alone. We all felt immediately guilty for having done that to our own parents for years, never thinking about what they did with their time alone in the park.

Meeting her opened my eyes. I decided I wanted to see what it was like to go to Disneyland by myself. I had the best time ever! The freedom was so exhilarating. I got to do all the things I wanted to do that my friends don't like. Since my favorite attraction is the Enchanted Tiki Room, this is actually an issue.

That solo visit to Disneyland taught me some amazing things. Doing things by yourself allows you to meet people you would never otherwise meet. The freedom you experience is truly inspiring.

My Advice

Accept that you are a dork. Understand that everyone else around you is a dork. Don't allow petty, mediocre people who try to pretend that they aren't dorks convince you to abandon your true self in order to gain acceptance. Allow yourself free expression and you will find the acceptance of truly exceptional people. Remember: dorks are happy, dorks are interesting, and most importantly, dorks are cool.

The main reason to shed your fears and allow yourself to be a dork is that people who accept that they are dorks and revel in their dorkiness are amazingly content. How can they not be when they are so happy? Free yourself from your fears, learn to be compassionate with the dorky mistakes you make, apply a good dose of self-deprecating humor, and you will find that you won't allow anyone to put a damper on your unbridled happiness ever again.

Being a Happy Humanist

> *"I was free – free to think, to express my thoughts . . . free*
> *to live for myself and those I loved . . . free to investigate, to*
> *guess and dream and hope."*
>
> *- Robert Ingersoll*

If you want to be happy, you need to free yourself from the limitations we all tend to put on ourselves. No one else can help us be happy. You have to take that responsibility for yourself. Humanists are some of the dorkiest and consequently happiest people I have ever met. Heck, the symbol for our philosophy is called the happy human.[2] Humanists are fairly intelligent people who revel in learning new and admittedly dorky things. We love to sit around telling really dorky jokes, and have long since stopped trying to fit in with people who refuse to understand us. It is quite liberating and inspiring to be amongst such people.

---

[2] If you get buried in a military cemetery, you can get a happy human on your tombstone.

Reality-based Decision Making

"Your focus determines your reality."
- *Qui-Gonn Jinn (Jedi Knight, in* Star Wars *Episode 1)*

Humanism concerns itself with finding human solutions to human problems. If you need to water your field, the most effective way is to irrigate it. You can, of course, pray for rain if you want. But most people will agree that irrigating your field is not only going to be more effective, but also more reliable.

In the pursuit of solving our problems, Humanists prefer to rely on what I like to call "reality-based decision making." The more you understand what is really causing the problems you are facing, the more effective your solutions will be. This might seem obvious, but the number of people who make decisions based on faulty assumptions about the root causes of their problems is astounding. Gut responses have their place in the heat of the moment, but there is usually enough time to do a little bit of research to find out if your assumptions are correct before you make any plans.

Problems caused by reality-free decision making are compounded for people who believe that there are supernatural forces at work, influencing their lives for better or worse. This isn't to say that supernatural forces aren't at work; it is just that people who believe their problems have supernatural origins tend to seek solely supernatural solutions.

Supernatural solutions have never been proven to be effective beyond a general placebo effect. I bring this up only because the seeking out of supernatural solutions to your problems might actually make matters worse.

Theological Non-science

> *"People are disturbed, not by things, but by the views they take of them."*
>
> *- Epictetus*

At some point in our lives we all go through something so stressful that all we want to do is skip forward and see how it all comes out. We obviously can't, but we certainly would have more peace of mind if we knew how things were going to turn out. It can be very tempting to seek out individuals who claim to be able to see the future or who claim to be able to seek supernatural assistance for your problem. Don't succumb to the temptation. You may buy a temporary respite for your mind, but your problems won't be solved and you would probably be better off spending that money on reality-based approaches to your problems.

Avoid all manner of psuedo-science and theological non-science. Psuedo-science can be defined as activities or areas of study that have the trappings of science but haven't actually been scientifically proven to be true. Most psuedo-sciences have a wealth of information and literature about them; people have studied them for years. Unfortunately, such studies are not objective or methodical and in most cases what is claimed by psuedo-scientists has no relationship to reality.

Astrology is a prime example of a psuedo-science. Astrologers look at star charts, and consult various ancient texts and other things to cast their fortunes. The problem is that not only has there been no real science to prove the validity of their claims, it turns out that the star charts they are using aren't accurate. Really.

Do yourself a favor. When tempted by anything that calls on a "sacred ancient wisdom" or appeals to the supernatural, find out what the skeptics have to say before you lay your money down. Being skeptical of claims isn't a negative thing. Think of it as a way to make sure your decisions are based in reality and that you don't give any of your hard-earned money to a charlatan.

Psychic Scams

The most common type of supernatural help sought by people in crisis is that of a psychic. What you need to know is that no one who claims to be a psychic has ever been able to prove that they are. It doesn't mean that they aren't psychic; it only means that no one who claims to be a psychic has been able to prove they have the skills they claim to have. This applies to all psychics.[3]

While there is nothing wrong with being open minded, consider this fact: several states have made it a crime to act as a psychic or fortuneteller for money. It is okay to do psychic readings for entertainment. It isn't okay to take money from vulnerable people by promising help you can't actually provide.

The main concern about using a psychic is that psychic scams are really common. While it is possible that people with psychic powers exist, most of the time, the people claiming to be psychics set up shop, bilk a large number of needy people out of large sums of money, and then skip town. The money taken in these scams are in the tens of thousands of dollars per person scammed. These scams are so common that it is best to err on the side of caution and assume that all psychics are out to scam you and avoid them entirely.

---

[3] There is actually a million dollar prize offered by the Randi Foundation to anyone who can prove "under proper observing conditions, evidence of any paranormal, supernatural, or occult power or event." From the James Randi Foundation Million Dollar Paranormal Challenge: http://www.randi.org/joom/challenge-info.html

If you want to go out and visit a psychic for the heck of it, go ahead and have fun. Just don't take them seriously if they tell you that you have an evil spirit hovering around you and that they can help make the evil spirit go away if you give them $5,000 to bless and bury in the ground near some sacred spot. And seriously, don't believe them when they tell you will get your money back in six weeks. Don't believe them if they say that all they are going to do is bless it and give it right back to you. They are skilled at switching envelopes. If a psychic starts saying things that scare you, ignore them. Let them search for another victim.

Medical Charlatans

When people get sick, especially with diseases that are hard to treat or are terminal, it is natural to seek out alternatives in hopes that you might be able to overcome the disease or even death. While some alternatives might be beneficial, many of these alternatives are scams. There might be a slight placebo effect, but the cost to purchase that placebo can be very, very high, especially if you ignore other, more traditional therapies as a result of getting that placebo. If you are going to seek out alternative therapies, find out if your state licenses them first. Whenever possible, seek out licensed professionals.

Some medical treatments that are considered alternative actually do have reasonable science behind them. These are the ones that the state will often license, such as Chinese medicine, acupuncture, acupressure, and massage therapy. These are not the sorts of alternative medicine prone to medical charlatanism though it is always a good idea to make sure you find reputable licensed practitioners. Even when licensed, there can be quacks.

The sorts of medical charlatanism I am warning about here include psychic surgeons, faith healers, regular psychics, and people working with crystals, psychic touch, homeopathy, and other bits of theological non-science. Again, be a skeptic and find out what the people who have looked into those claims have to say about the alternative treatment you are considering. You may be surprised by what you will find. For instance, it turns out that colon cleansing treatments that claim to rid your body of pounds of stuff stuck in your colon actually cause that gunk to build up inside you. Why would you do that to yourself? Find out the facts before you take an alternative treatment.

Paranormal medical practitioners have found ways to rationalize the fact that their claims are unproven, usually by saying that you have to believe in it for it to work. That is a convenient way to put the onus of failure on the patient rather than on the practitioner. The reality is that regardless of whether it seems scientific, if the claims are unproven it is theological non-science.

Take homeopathy for example. Don't be fooled by the fact you can buy homeopathic "remedies" in your local drug store. To put it politely, homeopathy is scientifically implausible. To be more direct, homeopathic products are indistinguishable from their placebo forms (water, sugar, alcohol, or cream). It would be cheaper to take a sugar pill. With homeopathy you have an untested theory that a substance that causes ills can be diluted until only the essence of the substance remains and that this extreme dilution will cure the problem that the original substance causes. I am not making this up. The homeopathy cure for headaches is actually caffeine, which is known to cause headaches. To make the placebo (by which I mean homeopathic medicine) you dilute caffeine into a solution so weak that if there is a single molecule of caffeine in a dose of the placebo it would be a miracle. Homeopathics claim it is ok if no molecules remain because the "essence" of it does, and no, I am not joking. Lots of people swear by homeopathy, but that is literally the placebo effect in action.

Skepticism Can Save Your Life

Most medical charlatanism is relatively harmless, generally providing a placebo effect for the patient. The worst that happens is that people spend their hard-earned money to buy false hopes. Unfortunately many practitioners of psychic treatments and medical charlatanism often encourage their victims (by which I mean patients) to forgo traditional medical treatments. To put this in really plain terms, medical charlatans might seem harmless but they have been known to cause the deaths of their victims. Don't be a victim. Ignore anyone claiming a miracle cure. If it sounds too good to be true, it probably is. Best to look to more established and traditional forms of medicine for help. If you are sticking to traditional forms of medicine, still do your research. Especially given the side effects of commonly prescribed drugs these days.

Putting it into Practice

Since reality-based decision making is so much more effective than the alternatives, the biggest question you need to ask yourself is how do to figure out what is real and what isn't. The best truth filter we humans have ever invented is science. Learn it, love it, and use it as a tool to help you figure out what is real and what isn't. The great thing about science is that you can devise your own experiments on the fly.

One of the quickest and easiest experiments you can do is the "ignore it and see if it goes away" test. This has many uses, and can help you deal with everything from minor annoyances to bullies and questions you may have about all manner of things supernatural. The basic premise of this method is that if something is real or really important, if you ignore it, it won't go away. Anything that does go away either wasn't real or wasn't really worth worrying about in the first place.

Hiding Under the Covers

> *"Fear is the main source of superstition, and one of the main sources of cruelty. To conquer fear is the beginning of wisdom."*
>
> *- Betrand Russell*

Think back to when you were a child. If you had a bad dream or if you convinced yourself that there was a monster under your bed, your best defense was usually to hide under the covers and pretend to ignore it. Eventually you would fall back asleep and wake up in the morning feeling fine. Hiding under the covers is a classic "ignore it and it will go away" method of dealing with a problem. While this might seem cowardly, there are many instances where this is a valid strategy that will help you conquer your fears and ensure that your decisions are firmly based in reality.

The Occult

The most important area to apply "ignore and it will go away" is anything dealing with the occult or the supernatural. Ghosts fall into this category and if you ever hid under the covers as a child, you already know how effective that strategy really is. This approach works for every supposedly negative supernatural influence that might be out there.

While I will reserve comment on whether there are or aren't ghosts or demons haunting our world, I will tell you this: people who don't believe in them never experience them. This is either because they are right that such things don't exist, or if they do exist, it turns out that if you ignore them, they really do go away.

Why am I telling you this? Because people who get involved with the occult waste an amazing amount of time, money, and energy freaking themselves out, spending money on unnecessary accoutrements, and losing their jobs and their friends. It is one thing to enjoy the occasional movie or ghost story; it is another thing entirely to spend your time and money looking for these things.

Don't Let the Devil In

To put it another way, if these spirits exist (which they probably don't) and if these spirits are in any way negative, why on earth would anyone invite them in? In literature on the subject, evil has to be invited into your house. You have to go looking for it. The devil can't harm you without your permission, so, don't give it permission.

I met a man once who admitted to me that he had done that. He was sitting on his porch at a secluded house in the country. He decided to ask for a sign that Satan really existed. Well, he got a sign and it scared the crap out of him. He made a mental note to never do that again. And, surprise surprise, he hasn't had any problems since.

I have another friend who used to be an honest to goodness occultist. He literally used to wake up at night and be convinced he was doing battle with some demon he couldn't see. He has since given up this sort of activity and as a result he has not been bothered by demons and ghosts since. Coincidence? I think not. He still believes that these things exist, but has adopted an "ignore it and it will go away" strategy that has been very effective for him. The biggest benefit seems to be that the energy he was spending on dealing with demons is now being spent on advancing his career and his relationships, which are now flourishing. Really, when it comes to the occult, you will be much happier if you ignore it.

Dealing with Obnoxious People

> *"There is nothing so aggravating as a fresh boy who is too old to ignore and too young to kick. "*
>
> *- Kin Hubbard*

"Ignore it and it will go away" has other, more secular applications than dealing with the occult and supernatural. It turns out that when dealing with obnoxious people, if you ignore them they will go away too. My mom always said, it takes two to fight and she was right. Bullies are looking for a response. If you don't respond to them, they will go away. Trust me on this.

Protecting Yourself

Obviously, if you need to do something to defend yourself, do so. You always want to protect yourself first and foremost. Remember to think before you act. If you need to pay attention to what someone is doing in order to protect yourself, simply pay attention to what they are doing while you pretend you are ignoring them and it will have the same effect as if you actually are ignoring them. They won't know the difference. This same strategy works for stalkers, in case you are ever stalked. Pay attention, but outwardly ignore them.

If ignoring the obnoxious person or bully isn't working, give it some more time. Often an individual will escalate their behavior in an effort to get a response. If you can ride that out without responding to them, they will eventually go away. Sometimes when the individual in question is seriously self-obsessed, it may take a little longer for them to realize they are being ignored and for them to move on in search of more productive prey. This strategy can take longer to work than some other more direct strategies, but it is more effective in the long run.

A Simple Caveat
If a bully or other person is actually physically assaulting you, do what you need to do to protect yourself. Your goal is to get away as safely as possible. If you aren't able to simply walk away, you may need to use force. Morally, you have the right to use force only to extract yourself from a dangerous situation. Self-defense classes are very useful in this regard. They can teach you how to handle different situations to keep yourself safe and how to apply judicious use of force so that you can get away.

Reality-based Decision Making

> *"Reality isn't the way you wish things to be, nor the way they appear to be, but the way they actually are."*
> - Robert J. Ringer

To be really effective at solving your problems, you need accurate information on what your problems are and the most effective ways to solve them. This is why Humanists encourage people to be skeptical of any and all claims. Find real solutions to your problems and don't be suckered in by people trying to make a fast buck at your expense. Fortunately, in this day and age, information on the various sorts of paranormal and psychic scams is easily found. While we are all tempted to fall victim to such scams, if you do a little bit of research, you can avoid the worst of them. This is especially important to do if something sounds scientific. Do your research and find out if it really is scientific and can be validated, or if it is just another form of theological non-science.

This does take a bit of critical thinking on your part, but the rewards for doing your research to find out the validity of claims is well worth the effort. It isn't enough to look at a list of people extolling the virtues of a given technique. You must look at the critiques as well.

Remember, being skeptical does not mean being a pessimist. It is just as bad to only look at critiques of a particular claim. You need to look at the claims both for and against whatever it is you are thinking critically about. Use the scientific method to help you figure out which side is most valid before coming to a conclusion.

For Example

Many people in the name of skepticism look only at one side of an argument. They assume that because they have looked for the negative in something that they are being skeptical. Nothing could be further from the truth. An example of this is the anti-vaccine movement. Most anti-vaccine opponents are well-educated individuals who encourage people to be skeptical about the safety of vaccines. Unfortunately, they forgot to use science. Not only does it turn out that vaccines do not cause autism, if enough people refuse vaccinations our herd protection is diminished and as a result many previously rare diseases are making a comeback. All because some well-meaning skeptics ignored the science and forgot that they need to consider both pro and con sides of any argument.

Is it easy? No. However, being skeptical means being optimistic that there is a solution to your problem and being proactive in finding a solution that will really solve your problem, and not empty promises and an empty pocketbook.

Keep it Simple, Stupid

"One is happy as a result of one's own efforts once one knows the necessary ingredients of happiness: simple tastes, a certain degree of courage, self denial to a point, love of work, and above all, a clear conscious. Happiness is no vague dream, of that I now feel certain."

— *George Sand*

This chapter is about simplicity. The title is taken from the acronym KISS, which stands for Keep It Simple, Stupid. It is a reminder to, well, keep it simple. My father taught me the KISS principle. My father is quoted twice in the book *Murphy's Law,* so his common sense is quite good. Originally my dad taught me this principle as it is applies to writing. But like all simple yet complex things, the KISS principle can be applied to other aspects of our lives. KISS is a key to happiness.

Sometimes it is the simple things that have the biggest impact. Humanism is a case in point. Humanism is actually a very simple philosophy. Yet, it has had a tremendous impact on the modern world. Humanism is one of the most powerful forces for positive social change on our planet. Yet the philosophy can be summed up simply: be a good person.

Say What?

"We need men with moral courage to speak and write their real thoughts, and to stand by their convictions, even to the very death."

- *Robert Green Ingersoll*

The primary application of KISS is in writing and other forms of communication. Your goal is to be easily understood.

An Example

When I was in college I was asked to read an essay by a respected linguist. I had an incredibly hard time sorting out what the man was trying to say. I finally decided to parse the sentence for structure – and yes, that skill does occasionally come in handy in the real world. What I found out was that even though this gentleman was using English words, he wasn't using English grammar. The problem with understanding his writing wasn't with me. It was entirely his fault. It isn't enough to choose the right words, you must also use grammar that can be understood and doesn't trip people up. In this case, I simply couldn't understand what was written because the author couldn't be bothered to include things such as verbs in his sentences.

Like the author mentioned above, we are all guilty of wanting to appear smart. We are forever tempted to use language that will make us seem smarter. Unfortunately, using big multisyllabic words, convoluted sentence structures, and other forms of obfuscation usually causes message failure.

Self Editing

KISS reminds us that the question you need to ask yourself is do you want act like you are smart, or do you want to be understood? Generally speaking it is better to be understood. A good rule of thumb when writing is to keep in mind your audience. Is what you are writing for general consumption? Or is it for a specialized group? If it is for the general public then you need to write so a fourth-grader can understand you. Smaller words with fewer syllables and short sentences are best.

Run your writing past several trusted colleagues and friends for feedback. The best writers all rewrite their work. Proofreading is imperative. There are some really cool programs on the Web now that will allow you to test your writing for simplicity to see if you are living up to this ideal. Use them and learn from them.

Constructive Criticism

Do not treat constructive criticism as an attack on your work. When people have questions, it is because they do not understand what you are trying to say. Your goal is to be clear, not to confuse. Use constructive criticism as an opportunity to clarify your work. Don't be afraid to completely revise if necessary. Above all, do not shoot the messenger! If you attack people you have asked to review your work, you will quickly run out of people willing to help you.

No Lies!

> *"Honesty is the best policy. If I lose mine honor, I lose myself."*
>
> *- William Shakespeare*

KISS is also a warning not to lie. Lying only makes your life more complicated. You might see a short-term gain in lying, but you can never totally avoid responsibility for your actions. Everything you do has consequences. Are you willing to pay the price for lying? The biggest price of lying is increased stress that you will be found out, and the ruining of your reputation and relationships when you are. Lying is not conducive to happiness.

Another cost of lying is that liars are incapable of having really good people as friends. Good people do not consider liars worthy of their friendship. Liars can only become friends with other liars. If you are hanging out with untrustworthy people, you will always be disappointed in them and will not be happy.

Finally, everyone knows lying is wrong. If you are lying, for whatever reason you have given yourself to justify your lies, you are letting yourself down. One of the primary elements of happiness is having a clear conscious. Do yourself a favor: keep is simple. Only stupid people lie.

What's in Your Food?

> *"Red meat is not bad for you. Now blue-green meat, that's bad for you!"*
>
> *- Tommy Smothers*

KISS also applies to your food choices. The simpler the food, the better it probably is for you. Get in the habit of reading food labels and try not to eat anything with extra ingredients. One time I was shopping with my husband and he wanted some fancy low-calorie orange juice that was more expensive than our normal brand. I made him compare the labels. My cheap orange juice had orange juice in it, nothing else. His fancy low-cal orange juice had orange juice and a slew of other unnecessary chemical ingredients in it. It should come as no surprise that the simple one is actually better for you. I personally try not to eat things with ingredients I don't recognize.

...or some reason sugar is one of the hardest ingredients to find in store-bought food. Most manufacturers like to substitute high-fructose corn syrup (HFCS) for sugar since it is cheaper and has preservative properties that give their products a longer shelf life. Whenever possible buy food without HFCS in it. HFCS does not act like sugar or taste like sugar, and its preservative properties have some unintended side effects. For example, bread made with HFCS is harder to toast then bread made with sugar. If you want decent toast that will crisp without having to be sent through the toaster repeatedly, you need to buy bread made with sugar or molasses and other easily identified ingredients and without preservatives and/or HFCS.

Peanut Butter

Another example of applying KISS to your food is peanut butter. The only ingredients that should be in peanut butter are peanuts and salt (which is optional). Look at your favorite brand. It probably is made with hydrogenated vegetable oil and some sort of sweetener. Peanuts rarely make an appearance in most of the popular brands. Once again you have a choice. You can have real peanut butter that not only tastes better but is better for you or you can have a peanut flavored spread that has a whole bunch of stuff you probably shouldn't be putting into your body and that tastes so bland it has to be sweetened with dangerous artificial sweeteners to make it palatable. Choose wisely.

Go Generic

Finally, check out a store's generic brands and compare the ingredients list with similar name brand products. Not only will you find that the generics are cheaper, they are generally made with much simpler and more real ingredients as well. Once you start keeping it simple with your food, you will never go back.

Simplicity Is Bliss

> "Life is really simple, but we insist on making it complicated. "
>
> > *- Confucius*

I started off this chapter with a quote from George Sand. In two places she notes that "simple tastes" and "self-denial to a point" are part of her recipe for happiness. Both of these along with flexibility are in important when applying KISS principles to daily life.

Simple Tastes

There are several reasons why KISS should be applied to your daily life. First, simple tastes are much easier to acquire. The reason for this should be obvious. If you don't need a huge mansion with a swimming pool, then you will probably be quite happy with whatever housing you end up with. People with simple tastes really are happier than people with expensive tastes.

People who have extravagant tastes are always searching for the next best thing and are rarely satisfied with what they have. This is obviously expensive and a great way to become poor. But there is another hidden danger. Always trying to buy bigger and better things is like having an addiction that can never be satisfied. Doesn't sound like too much fun, does it? Best to be happy with what you have.

Self Denial—to a Point

Having simple tastes does not mean Spartan living, although that is fine for some. This is why Sand says that self-denial is only good to a point. Obsessively adhering to any set of principles is unhealthy. Flexibility is key.

As Benjamin Franklin pointed out, everything should be done in moderation. If you can afford something nice and you really want it, go ahead and get it. When I bought my house, I splurged on a really nice sofa. I love my sofa. It was more expensive and nicer than I needed, but I love it and it makes me happy. I did the same thing with my fridge. I spent an extra $200 and got one with an icemaker and water in the door that was bigger than the cheaper one. I was planning to own this fridge for more than ten years, so the extra cost up front was totally worth it to me.

Flexibility

I learned the importance of being flexible with my simple tastes from a budget travel guide, which goes to show you that wisdom can be found anywhere. In this book, the author talked about how budget-conscious travelers need to splurge on a nice hotel room now and again to remind themselves that they are human. Too much pinching of pennies will cause you to lose your sense of reality. Splurging every now and again is ok. Be conscious of costs, but the point of traveling and living is to enjoy yourself, and splurging now and then is fun and helps make sure your memories are happy ones.

A Cautionary Tale: Scrimping Gone Bad

When I was going to school in China, one of my fellow foreign students had gotten to Shanghai via third-class ticket from Guangdong. He could have spent about $2 more to get a first-class ticket, but he wanted to save his money. His third-class ticket meant he had to sit on a hard bench, crowded in with throngs of other people for a three-day trip. In other words, the cost of saving $2 was to not sleep for three full days.

If he had spent the extra $2, he would have had a private berth and could have not only gotten some solitude, but he also would have been able to sleep lying down, quite literally saving his sanity. The folks that knew him in the United States before he took that trip all said that he was never quite right in the head after riding that train.

Don't let this happen to you. Keep your tastes simple, but treat yourself now and again. Remember, all things in moderation goes both ways. Simple tastes and self-denial can help you be happy, but only to a point! So remember to be flexible and take the opportunity to treat yourself every now and again.

Do Not Keep Up with the Joneses

> *"I'm living so far beyond my income that we may almost be said to be living apart."*
>
> *- e. e. cummings*

Whether you are still in school, out of college, starting out in life, or well into your retirement, you will notice that some people always seem to be able to afford whatever they want. They can take vacations to cool places, buy expensive new clothes, and always seem to have the latest, neatest toys. Put simply, they never seem to worry about money. These people are popularly known as the Joneses. Do not try to keep up with them.

It is important to realize that trying to keep up with the Joneses is a sure-fire way to make yourself extremely unhappy. First, everyone has different financial situations. Dealing productively with the reality of your fiscal situation is emotionally healthy. Pretending you have money you don't is not. Second, there is a very high likelihood that the Joneses are living beyond their means and are digging themselves a very deep financial hole. Do not follow them into that hole.

Debt-free Living

It is best to learn as soon as possible to live within your means. Financial stress from out-of-control debt is so horrible, it can actually end otherwise happy marriages. The easiest way to become financially well off is to not spend your money paying off debts. To do this you need to learn to only buy things you can actually afford.

Living debt free means that the money you would otherwise be spending on interest payments can actually go into savings. And yes, there are people out there who are debt free. My mother bought her last car with cash. My husband and I only have debt on our two properties and one car that we are paying off early so that we can minimize our interest payments.

Interest payments are money you give to someone else for the pleasure of spending their money instead of your own. Depending on the interest rate, it could increase the cost of an item dramatically. My husband and I saw a commercial for a payday advance with an interest rate of 100 percent. That means if you borrow $100, you need to pay back $200. So, instead of buying what you were going to buy for $100, you actually paid $200 for it. That is just plain stupid!

The Bare Necessities

> *"To be happy with simple pleasures is no simple matter."*
> *- Unknown*

The key to living debt free is to understand what you can actually afford, and that means budgeting. So I hope you paid attention in math class, as those skills define the difference between those who are financially stable and those who aren't.

A budget lists not only your income, but also your expenses and your estimated expenses. If your expenses are more than your income, you have a problem. Ideally, you want a budget that has you spending less than what you earn; that way you can save some too.

Every month you will find you have some fixed expenses. These are things such as housing, transportation, food, utilities, and medical expenses. These are the bare necessities. Other things such as recreation, miscellaneous entertainment and gifts, etc. are discretionary, which means, if push comes to shove, you can do without them.

Reality-based Home Economics

Rough guidelines are readily available on what percentage of your income should be spent on each of the bare necessities. These guidelines are extremely useful, as they will help you understand what it is you can actually afford so that you don't end up going into debt. And yes, it does mean you will need to rely on simpler tastes, especially when you are getting started on your own. You will also need to know basic math skills to translate these percentages into real numbers based on your monthly income.

Ignore your budget and you may find yourself in financial peril. If you spend too much on housing and transportation so you can have something flashy, you may not be able to afford food, medical care, or that vacation you want to take. Everything has a trade-off. And yes, the Joneses always seem to be able to afford everything they want. You aren't one of those Joneses and should not try to be.

As a general rule you should try to spend less than 30 percent of your income on housing. Any more than that and you will start cutting into your other necessities and your discretionary spending might have to be eliminated entirely. Zero discretionary spending makes for a very dull life. Transportation (e.g., your car loan and insurance payments, gas, and maintenance) should only be about 18 percent of your budget. Given the fact that gas prices tend to fluctuate wildly, this can be very hard to do. But if you have to get a bus pass to do this, then that is what you need to do. 16 percent generally goes to food. 5 percent goes to medical insurance and bills. 5 percent goes to utilities, 5 percent to recreation, 5 percent to clothing, and the rest to debt payments if you have them, or savings if you don't.

The key is that regardless of the categories within your budget, the total percentage of your budget should only add up to 100 percent. You can and should add in a category for contingency savings as well as categories for other high-cost things you are planning to pay for in the future such as travel, holiday shopping, or other high-cost items you may want to purchase. My mother has a budget item for future cars so she puts away a bit every month to pay for a new car in cash when she is ready to buy one. Remember to subtract from other areas to make sure your budget adds up properly.

Sticking to Your Plan

This might seem like a drag, but you will be happier if you stay within your budget and base your budget on real numbers. Do you really need that flashy car, or would you rather take a vacation? These are the types of questions you should be asking yourself every time you go to buy something.

It may seem to you like everyone is keeping up with the Joneses, and that might be true of the people around you. But smart, happy people aren't trying to keep up. They make their budgets and stick to them, and retire happy because they kept their finances in line with their income and were actually able to enjoy themselves and save some money at the same time.

Is it easy to stick with your budget? No, you do have to deny yourself to a point, as George Sand points out. But keeping it simple will go a long way to making it easier. Simple tastes mean simple finances. Simple finances mean a simple life and that leads to happiness.

Contingency Plan

It is very important to plan for contingencies in your budget. While you may be working now, what would happen if you lost your job? Even if you have a good job, things happen. Cars break down, air conditioning units go out, and sometimes you have to evacuate your home in the case of an emergency.

Contingency planning affects your budget in two ways. First, when you are looking to purchase big-ticket items such as cars and houses, it is always good to make sure you don't spend too much, so if you do lose your job, you won't lose your home. When I bought my house, the bank offered to loan me twice as much money as I wanted to borrow. I stuck to my budget though. And now, I own a home I can afford if I were working at a minimum-wage job. I planned for a bad contingency and so when the markets turned down, I was not concerned about whether or not I would be able to keep my home.

The second way to plan for contingencies is to put money away for the proverbial rainy day. From a work perspective, you might want to have 3 to 6 months worth of income set aside in case you lose your job. That will provide you with a little bit of a buffer to give you time to find a replacement job without having to lose your home. One summer both my husband and I were out of work. While my exit from the workforce was planned, his was sudden. Despite the economic uncertainty that hung over us, we had a really fun summer. We were able to relax because we had budgeted for such an unforeseen situation. Though my husband was looking for work, we knew we had saved enough money to tide us over until he found one. At no point did I consider looking for a job myself. We simply cut back on some luxury items and reduced our expenses wherever we could. We weren't in any danger of losing our houses or cars. The most important thing that our buffer provided us was that it allowed my husband to find the right job for him and not take the first offer that came along.

It is also important to be putting money away for car maintenance, and perhaps have a plan for if you have to evacuate your home. How much money will you need and where will you be staying? Heck, I even own some euros as insurance against a precipitous decline in the dollar. Thinking through what might happen and planning for it isn't being a nervous Nelly, unless you take it to an extreme. Putting aside some money so you can afford to handle an emergency is simple common sense.

Using Debt Wisely

> "Money is better than poverty, if only for financial reasons."
>
> *- Woody Allen*

While living debt free is a noble goal, it is actually very important to build and maintain a good credit rating. There are things such as houses and cars that you will want to buy on credit, and the better your credit score is, the lower your potential interest payments will be. The lower your interest payments are, the less extra money you are paying for the privilege of borrowing the money and that is always a good thing. Unfortunately, the only way to build your credit score is to borrow money.

Borrow Only What You Can Afford

When I was in college, I was planning to buy a word processor / typewriter. And yes, this was before computers were readily available. Anyway, I had the cash to pay for it, as it was only a couple hundred dollars. My parents insisted that I take out a loan to buy it. I didn't understand it at the time, but buying that computer with a low-interest loan that I could easily and readily pay off helped me build up some credit. I was becoming a known entity to the banks. By purchasing a few judicious items through credit, items that I not only needed but also could actually afford with cash, I became a reliable borrower, which is something the banks love. When it came time to purchase my first car, I not only was easily approved for a car loan, I was given a great low rate.

Just Because They Offer It Doesn't Mean You Need to Take It

When I was talking to banks about home loans so I could buy my first house, I was actually offered twice the money I was asking for. I refused it. I wanted only a debt payment I could easily afford. If I had borrowed all the money they had offered me, I could have bought a bigger house, but the extra debt would have broken my budget. Just because someone is willing to lend you money doesn't mean you should borrow it. Know what you can afford and stick to it.

A lower payment on my house has also afforded my husband and me the luxury of not worrying about work. When push comes to shove, we know we can afford our house regardless of our work situation. There is a lot of freedom in that knowledge and with that freedom comes less stress. With less stress, we are happier. Stick to what you know you can afford and resist the temptation to borrow money just because it is offered.

Zero-interest Loans

A great way to build credit is to take advantage of zero-interest loans for things you need to buy anyway. The important thing to remember is to not borrow more than you can easily pay off before the date the interest starts accruing. The banks are betting that you won't pay off this sort of loan on time and so, when the zero-interest period ends; it is usually followed by a high interest rate. Make sure you pay off this sort of loan well before any interest starts accruing, otherwise your zero-interest loan will become a very expensive loan, which is not something you ever want to deal with.

Credit Cards

Credit cards are a necessary evil. You will need a credit card for emergencies. I learned this the hard way when I was traveling in China as a young woman. I literally didn't have enough money to get home, but my mother was able to wire $300 to Hong Kong, which tided me over until the end of my trip. If I had had a credit card, I would not have needed to bother her and risk getting stuck literally on the other side of the world. As soon as I got home, I applied for a card.

Credit cards come in handy in emergencies, but that is how you should use them: for emergencies only. Do not rack up debt simply to purchase things you cannot otherwise afford. This is how people get into trouble. I keep my credit card in the house and only use it occasionally. I use my debit card for all other purchases. I am not tempted to spend money I don't have. My husband, who fortunately has a financial ethic similar to mine, keeps his cards in the freezer so he isn't tempted to use them unless absolutely necessary.

When you do use a credit card, try to pay off the entire debt as soon as possible, ideally in the next billing period. Generally, you only have to pay interest on a credit card loan if you float that debt for more than a month. So, if you pay it off promptly, you will not have any interest payments. If you have to, you can break the payback into two or three payments, and incur minimal interest. Make sure you pay off those cards quickly. Otherwise you are giving your money away to a bank and that is money that would be better spent on you.

at you never want to do is pay the minimum balance allowed on your credit card bill. Unfortunately, this is what a lot of people do and they end up spending way more for the things they buy on credit than the original purchase price would have cost them.

Apparently, they never paid attention in math class and/or never learned to read the fine print. Everything has a cost. Moneylenders make their money from the interest. The longer you take to pay off the principal debt, the more money they make through your interest payments. Using debt wisely means minimizing your interest payments or eliminating them entirely.

Playing the Moneylenders

Moneylenders are essentially gamblers. The more people that borrow money from them and the more people there are that don't pay off debts promptly, the more lenders get to increase their precious interest payments.

It turns out that the less money you borrow from a lender and the less interest you pay to them, the more they will lower interest rates for you in an effort to entice you to borrow money from them, in hopes that you will make a mistake and pay them some interest. After all, some interest is better than none and they know that while some people are smart enough to refuse to pay high interest rates, most aren't. You want to be in the too-smart-to-pay-interest category. This requires you to only borrow what you can actually afford.

Of course, if you never borrow money, they will stop offering you low interest rates altogether, so be sure to use a credit card at least once a year, ideally when you are purchasing something you know you can pay off within the next month. That is the best way to ensure that credit is there should you ever need it.

KISS

> "If I told you what it takes to reach the highest high, you'd
> laugh and say 'nothing's that simple.'"
> - The Who ("I'm Free" from the rock opera
> Tommy)

Make "Keep It Simple, Stupid" your mantra. Apply it to your work, your writing, your lifestyle, your finances, your relationships, and your philosophy. It is always amazing to me when I hear how otherwise sane people convolute and confuse the simplest situations. I sometimes suspect people think that if something is too simple, it can't be right.

The KISS approach is backed up by science. Well, scientists, philosophers, and logicians anyway. Most people are familiar with the principle of Occam's razor, which states that all things being equal, the simpler solution is probably the best solution. This is true of many things in life, yet we routinely ignore this wisdom and try to make things more complicated than they really are.

I have seen this with people I have taught to dance who refuse to believe that swing dancing is as easy as it really is. I have seen it with students I have mentored in math who refuse to believe that the math they are learning is as easy as it appears to be and instead prefer to believe there is something they are missing. And I have seen it with people who are looking for a life philosophy that can help them succeed in their lives.

Humanism is very simple. Be a good person. That's it. It doesn't take any mental gymnastics to practice. There is no contradicting dogma. There are no complex rituals to learn. Just, be a good person.

If you are currently searching for a philosophy that can help you succeed in life and are being drawn in by religions or practices that require you to engage in serious mental gymnastics because things don't make sense or, worse, violate your internal sense of moral justice, you need to stop what you are doing. You don't need to follow some convoluted path that requires you to believe nonsense or conduct some nonsensical ritual. Try your best to be a good human being, stay firmly based in reality, practice compassion, keep it simple, and you will do just fine.

When Pete Townsend wrote "I'm Free" for *Tommy*, he may not have been aware at just how profound his song is. Because it speaks to a basic Humanist truth, I am providing the complete lyrics below.

I'm free -- I'm free,
And freedom tastes of reality!
I'm free -- I'm free,
And I'm waiting for you to follow me.
If I told you what it takes
To reach the highest high,
You'd laugh and say "Nothing's that simple."
But you've been told many times before
Messiahs pointed to the door
And no one had the guts to leave the temple!
I'm free -- I'm free,
And I'm waiting for you to follow me.
I'm free -- I'm free,
And I'm waiting for you to follow me.

It's Your Body

"Take care of yourself. Good health is everyone's major source of wealth. Without it, happiness is almost impossible."

- Unknown

Humanists want to live long and happy lives. Most Humanists you meet are hoping to live to be a supercentenarian (110+) and would take immortality if it were offered. When you are enjoying life, you want to have as much of it as you can get.

Regarding longevity, you may not have realized this but the number of centenarians (people over 100) has risen dramatically in the past two decades. When I was growing up, it was amazing if someone lived to be 100. Now it is fairly commonplace and we only really get excited when we learn about supercentenarians. In 2007 and 2008, more than 150 people were certified as supercentenarians, with the oldest dying at the age of 116 in early 2008. The likelihood that more and more of us will live to such ripe old ages is getting better. It is important to start thinking about what sort of health you would like to be in when you reach that age. Many of these supercentenarians lived independently well into their 100s. You would be wise to plan to as well.

If you want to live a long and happy life, you must live a healthy life. Unhealthy people simply don't live long enough to qualify as having had a long life by Humanist standards. Plus, it's kind of hard to enjoy life to the fullest when you are sick or in pain.

Because it is so important to take care of your body, this chapter is devoted to helping you understand your body and your health. What follows are some basic rules of thumb that you should know but may not have been told. And please be aware that these are rough guidelines. No suggestion should be taken as absolute, and always check with your doctor.

You Weigh How Much?

"The good Lord gave you a body that can stand most anything. It's your mind you have to convince."

- Vincent Lombardi

Being overweight or underweight is unhealthy. Overweight people don't usually live as long as healthy people. They have more health problems and more potentially life-threatening problems. Being underweight also causes problems. Your goal is to maintain a healthy weight.

This is easier said than done because society conspires to distort our self-image. Very few people like what they see in the mirror, mostly because they don't look like the images of perfection they see on TV and at the movies.

What You Need to Know

Nowadays, famous people and models are almost all underweight. Some are downright sickly looking. Do not feel that you have to be wafer thin or ripped with muscles to be attractive. Don't develop an eating disorder because of a poor self-image. If you are too skinny, or are focused on being too skinny, you can develop severe health problems and possibly die. You would be better off looking at movies and TV shows filmed in the 1950s to get a better idea of what a healthy, normal body looks like.

For girls, take a good long look at Marilyn Monroe. She was not skinny, and yet she was considered extremely sexy. Take a look at paintings of women from the Renaissance. These women look absolutely "fat" by today's standards, but in reality, they are what healthy women should look like.

For us girls, what really matters is not how much you weigh, or how flat your stomach is, but is your hip to waist ratio. According to modern research, men from every corner of the globe and every culture find curves attractive. Curves require a minimum level of plumpness. Believe it or not, real men find your belly bump adorable.

The same rule applies to men. Look at the sex symbols of the 1950s who showed off their bodies. Tarzan comes to mind. He didn't have six-pack abs. He wasn't ripped. He was, however, fit, and quite a good-looking man. Basically, as long as you aren't flabby and don't have a beer belly, you are probably okay.

Healthy Living

How will you know if you are a healthy weight? Check with your doctor, or check your body mass index (BMI) against a reliable health chart, which takes into account your age and sex. If you think you are too fat or too skinny, consult with your doctor and find out if you really are, or just think you are.

Keeping a healthy weight is relatively simple. Despite all the fad diets, it comes down to this: eat healthy foods in moderate portions and exercise regularly. Healthy foods are less refined than unhealthy foods. When in doubt, make it yourself. Pumpkin pie is easy to make from a real pumpkin and won't have all the chemical junk in it. Same with ice cream, which normally contains cream, sugar, and a touch of salt, plus whatever fruit or flavoring you want to put in it. I have found that, in general, it takes me about the same amount of time to cook a healthy dinner from scratch as it does to cook pre-packaged meals. And it is a lot less expensive and a lot healthier. So, do yourself a favor and learn how to cook.

Did You Save Room for Dessert?

> "Don't wreck a sublime chocolate experience by feeling guilty."
>
> *- Lora Brody*

Dieting is all about portion control. Eat less and exercise more. Unfortunately, in America, our sense of portion is really out of skew. I have adopted a "save room for dessert" strategy to eating. In the old days, people used to eat a lot of pie, and they weren't fat. The reason for this is because they were eating more rational portions of food. It isn't the dessert that makes you fat; it is how much you eat and what you eat.

If You Feel Stuffed, You've Eaten Too Much

Believe it or not, in Europe, you can get a seven-course meal and not feel stuffed at the end. Every course of the meal is small enough that you can enjoy it, but still have room for the next item, including dessert. And when you finish dessert, you feel good but not stuffed.

You could have a small salad, some veggies, starch, and some meat, and still have room for dessert. Keep your portions on the small size and enjoy a great meal including dessert. Remember to eat a balanced diet. If all you eat is dessert and junk food, you will not be healthy. Your body needs basic nutrients to function. Make sure you give it what it needs.

Use It or Lose It

> *"True enjoyment comes from activity of the mind and exercise of the body; the two are ever united."*
>
> *- Wilhelm von Humboldt*

Exercising your body will not only help keep you at a healthy weight, it can also help with your mental fitness. Human bodies are capable of doing some amazing things. The adage "Use it or lose it" applies here. If you want to be able to hike across Ireland some day, you will need to keep up your fitness level so that when the opportunity arises, your body will be up to the challenge. Do you want to bike across India? Make sure you keep your body fit and your heart in good shape.

I keep in shape because I like using my body. It is a joy to feel my muscles work, stretch, and strengthen doing everything from canoeing to hiking to dancing and stone carving. Having a strong body is a wonderful feeling and allows you to enjoy life's experiences better because you will not be doubled over in pain with a stitch in your side. So, use your body or lose it and don't become a couch spud. At the minimum, get outside and go for a walk at least once a day.

Sit Up Straight

> *"One of the best ways of improving how you feel about yourself and the world around you is to enhance your posture."*
>
> *- Noel Kingsley*

Your mama's admonition to sit up straight and pay attention to your posture is correct. Good posture has several benefits. First, people with good posture have less back pain than people who slouch. Anyone who suffers from back pain will tell you that avoiding it is worth your while. Plus, your body performs better when your posture is correct.

The second reason to sit up straight is because it makes you look more attractive. First impressions are important. People who slouch look unsure and insecure. People with good posture look confident, regal, and important. This is true for both men and women. If you don't believe me, look around you. Start paying attention to who has good posture and how you perceive them.

In order to have good posture, you must practice good posture. This isn't something you can pull off without practice. When you sit down to eat, check your posture. When you go for a walk, check your posture. When you are at the supermarket, don't hunch over the cart resting your arms on it. Stand up straight and push the cart with your hands. Whenever you think about it, check your posture. After a while it will become second nature to you to have good posture.

There are many ways to "visualize" your posture. One of the most common ways is to imagine a string coming up through your spine and through the top of your head. Imagine this string being pulled up and straightening your spine, lifting your head up a bit. Now, drop your chin (but not your head) and you are now probably standing up straight. Another way to achieve good posture is to throw your shoulders back and say, "I look cool." Then, tuck in your tummy, bend your knees slightly and drop your chin but not your head. Keep your head high like a string is pulling it up. And, again, your posture is probably good.

Don't stick your tummy out; if you do, no matter how broad you make your shoulders, you will have a sway back. That is not good posture, is not attractive, and can cause back problems. So, chest out, shoulders back, tummy in, knees slightly bent, chin down, head up, eyes straight ahead.

Water, Water Everywhere

> "Not all chemicals are bad. Without chemicals such as hydrogen and oxygen, for example, there would be no way to make water."
>
> - Dave Barry

Drinking water is a good way to ensure you stay healthy. If I get a headache, nine times out of ten it is because I am dehydrated. When I was pregnant, pretty much every ache, pain, and discomfort could be mitigated by drinking more water. This, in my opinion, is the single easiest thing you can do to keep yourself healthy.

How do you know if you are drinking enough? By the color of your urine. It should be pale yellow or clear. If it is not pale or clear, you need to drink more. However, the old adage "In all things, moderation" applies here. If you drink too much water without taking in salt, you can also cause an imbalance. But you would have to drink a whole lot of water to do that.

Also, as it turns out, the "eight glasses of water a day" rule isn't actually true. Drink when you are thirsty, and try not to drink things with refined sugar in them and you should be fine.

Take Pride in Your Poop

"Psychiatry's chief contribution to philosophy is the discovery that the toilet is the seat of the soul."

- Alexander Chase

Because proper bowel function is an essential part of your overall health, it is necessary to talk about poop. What you are looking for is a soft, solid sinker. If your poop floats, you are eating too much fat. If it is difficult to pass or looks like small rocks, then you are not getting enough water. If it is too loose, drink more water, seriously.

On a related topic, no bowel moves before its time, but when it's time, it's time. There isn't much you can do to hold things back. All you really need to do is get to an appropriate place and relax.

Relax

Your bowels work best when you don't spend a lot of time thinking about them. Thinking only interferes with what is supposed to be an automatic process, or, in other words, a process that doesn't require conscious thought to occur. Try to breathe while thinking about breathing and you will see what I mean.

What I am trying to say is don't force things. Forceful pushing only causes hemorrhoids or other injuries and you really don't want those. Forcing doesn't work anyway. Your bowels will empty when they are good and ready to and not a moment sooner. No bowel moves before its time.

Relaxation is especially important when you are constipated. I know it is hard to not tense up when things are, well, hard, but if you do manage to relax, things are more likely to come out all right on their own.

If you have trouble relaxing during the evacuation of your bowels, don't fret, that only makes things worse. The easiest remedy to too much thinking is to bring along reading material like everyone else does. Reading or doing a crossword puzzle should help you take your mind off things long enough to allow your body to go about its business uninterrupted by that pesky little brain of yours.

Be polite to everyone else in the world, and put the lid down before you flush so your nasty poop water doesn't splash all over the bathroom. And most of all, don't forget you need to wash your hands. "Wash, wash, you gotta wash your fingers. If you want to eat with them, you gotta wash them."[4]

---

[4] This is a song I sing for my son when we wash our hands.

Sleeping Beauty

"A good laugh and a long sleep are the two best cures in the doctor's book."
- Scottish proverb

There is a Descendents[5] song called "Thanks to Modern Chemistry, Sleep in Now Optional." Do not fall into this trap. Sleep deprivation can be an insidious thing and you might not realize that you are not getting enough sleep. It can impair your judgment and make you tired. Sleep deprivation can be used as a form of torture. Don't torture yourself.

Your body and mind will work much better with a full nights sleep. That means, at least 7 hours, preferably eight. Go to bed at a reasonable time and you will thank yourself for it in the morning. Living a happy healthy life requires you to be fully awake and aware to enjoy it.

Tossing and Turning

Probably the most important time to get a full night's sleep is when you have something important the next day that will require your mental faculties to be working at high efficiency. Unfortunately these are often the nights when it is hardest to get to sleep. If you are like me, your mind will start racing, perhaps worrying about how things are going to go.

In these situations, I like to meditate. Learning how to quiet your mind will help you shut your thoughts down and fall asleep. Try to avoid sleeping pills, especially the over-the-counter ones. These will put you to sleep, but you won't necessarily dream. If you sleep without dreaming, you will not feel rested when you wake up, so it is best to try the meditation and other methods of going to sleep on your own first.

If you have been through a significant emotional trauma and have not been able to get a decent night's sleep for some time, talk to your doctor about your sleeping problems. Your doctor might recommend something for the short term. Remember that your goal is to get yourself to sleep on your own. Keep trying to go to sleep without medical aids if you can. Follow your doctor's advice and don't become dependent on sleeping pills. Addictions are horrible things and really get in the way of having a happy, healthy life.

---

[5] LA punk band that started in the 1980s

<u>*Learn to Love Your Naps*</u>

One of the findings of modern science is that left to our own devices, without light cues, humans will sleep 6 hours at night and 2 hours during the day to get their full 8 hours of sleep. The *siesta* is a bona-fide good thing. Since most of us can't sleep during the day because of our work schedules, don't be afraid to take naps during the weekends. Or when you get home in the evening. Learn to love your naps.

In All Things, Moderation

> *"Moderation in all things, including moderation."*
> *- Benjamin Franklin*

You don't want to be too skinny, but you also don't want to be too fat. You don't want to eat too much, but you don't want to starve yourself either. Ben Franklin was right, in all things, moderation. This means that you will have to be responsible enough to use your brain to figure out what is right and not allow yourself to go overboard on any one thing. If you start obsessing about your weight, your poop, your piss, or how much sleep you are getting, you will not enjoy yourself. Take a deep breath, laugh at how much of a dork you are, and then go do something else.

When it comes to your health, you need to take all the above advice with a grain of salt. Use your own head and take responsibility for your own life and health. That is after all the Humanist approach to pretty much everything.

Just Say No

"Addiction is a symptom of not growing up. I know people think it's a disease . . . If you have a brain tumor, if you have cancer, that's a disease. To say that an addiction is a disease is not fair to the real diseases of the world."

- C. C. DeVille

Humanism, because it is an individualist philosophy, believes that people should have the right to engage in whatever behavior they think will increase their happiness, even if the majority considers a particular behavior to be bad or "sinful." You are free to pursue your happiness with only a few necessary restrictions. For example, you have the right to drink, but not the right to drive while drunk, which could negatively impact others.

What you need to know and understand before you set off is that not all pursuits end in happiness. This chapter is designed to help you choose your behaviors wisely by explaining how indulging in "sinful" behavior can get in the way of your happiness.

Happiness vs. Pleasure

"Happiness is not synonymous with pleasure. It is, instead, a deeper emotion that originates from within."

- David Shi

As humans, it is natural for us to seek pleasure. And there is nothing wrong with that. Be aware: pleasure is not the same thing as happiness. Pleasures are temporary and while they can feel good in the moment, they can be rather shallow emotionally. Happiness on the other hand, is deep and long lasting. Don't confuse the two.

We all know that we shouldn't drink, smoke, do drugs, have sex with strangers, etc. Yet, very few of us actually consider why there are society-wide prohibitions or restrictions on these activities. Whether or not you believe in "sin" in the religious sense, you should be aware that there are many real life reasons why these things came to be considered sins. The main reason is because, generally speaking, they won't make you happy.

Studies have shown that people who drink or use drugs are simply not as happy as those who don't. You can see this for yourself if you look around at your friends. Whether they drink because they are unhappy or they are unhappy because they drink makes little difference. The fact remains, they simply aren't all that happy.

Don't get me wrong; there is absolutely nothing immoral in partaking of simple pleasures. Go ahead and indulge on occasion. Just don't let your indulgences get in the way of pursuing happiness.

Problem Solving 101

> "Nobody really cares if you're miserable, so you might as well be happy."
>
> - Cynthia Nelms

The only way to achieve happiness is to take control of your life by dealing effectively with your problems. You can't solve your problems if you ignore them. Don't make the mistake of indulging in drugs, alcohol, or any other addictive substance as a way to avoid dealing with your problems. The longer you ignore a problem, the bigger and more oppressive it will be.

If you are really unhappy with how things currently are, there is nothing wrong with occasionally indulging in a pleasure to seek solace or to forget about it for a short time. However, the sooner you solve your problems the happier you will be.

Compounding Interest

> "The significant problems we face cannot be solved at the same level of thinking we were at when we created them."
>
> Albert Einstein

Do not compound your problems. It is hard enough dealing with what life throws at you. It is just plain stupid to compound your problems by adding easily avoidable problems to your list. By simply not indulging in "sinful" pleasures, you can reduce the number of problems you are dealing with dramatically.

For Example

Drinking isn't usually that harmful. But if you drink and drive because you aren't thinking clearly, then you could get a ticket, lose your license, get in an accident, lose your life or kill someone else. If you thought the original problem was difficult enough to cope with, try dealing with it while in traction.

Spending Your Time Wisely

> *"Most people spend more time and energy going around problems than in trying to solve them."*
>
> *- Henry Ford*

Another reason why indulging in so-called sinful behavior will not help you be happy is because you only have so much time and energy to spend every day. Instead of spending your time drinking, doing drugs, or playing video games for hours on end, all because you would rather not think about your job, grades, living situation, love life, or whatever, do something to improve your life. If you don't like your job, find another one. If your grades are bad, playing video games isn't going to change that. The only way out of a bad relationship is to get out of it. And yes, all these examples should be perfectly obvious to anyone who spends even a smidgeon of time thinking about them. But most people don't, so it isn't. Don't make that mistake. Think about what you want to accomplish and then spend your time working towards your goals.

Peer Pressure

> *"He alone is great and happy who requires neither to command nor to obey in order to secure his being of some importance in the world."*
>
> *- Johann Wolfgang Von Goethe*

One of the biggest reasons why people indulge in things they know better than to do is peer pressure. Resisting peer pressure takes a lot of courage. However, there is a very easy technique that you can use that will help you resist this sort of pressure and that is to label peer pressure properly.

A Courageous Exercise

People engaging in peer pressure try to make it seem like there is something wrong with you if you don't go along with them. The real stigma should be on the inappropriate attempt to manipulate people through peer pressure. The technique my friends and I used when we were in high school was to yell out "PEER PRESSURE!" whenever someone attempted to influence us in this way. It drew negative attention to the individual doing the pressuring and, thus, took pressure off us to yield. The sheer act of yelling "PEER PRESSURE!" in a crowded hallway will earn you the respect of others for being courageous enough to resist.

Being Sociable

"It is better to hide ignorance, but it is hard to do this when we relax over wine."

— *Heraclitus*

Most of the time, peer pressure isn't obvious. It is the unspoken and tacit acceptance of behaviors that can lead you astray. If you are at a party and everyone is drinking, then it is pretty obvious that you are expected to drink as well. The problem is that some people do not know how to moderate their drinking.

My mother taught me how to navigate these sorts of social situations, and that is by indulging a little. If everyone is drinking and you want to be sociable, go ahead and get a drink, preferably one that isn't too hard, then nurse it all evening. Trust me on this one; people don't pay much attention to how much others are drinking. They want to feel like it is ok to drink and so, by having a drink in your hand, you are allowing others to feel like they aren't being judged, and that is part of what being sociable is all about.

Drinking Responsibly

"The first drink with water, the second without water, the third like water."

— *Spanish maxim*

Being drunk isn't pleasant. A simple buzz is quite enough and should be what you are aiming for anyway. Anything more than that is unpleasant and could cause other problems, which you would be smart to avoid. Fortunately, it doesn't take much to achieve a slight buzz. Learn how to drink responsibly.

One Drink

Set your mind to only have one drink for your night out and then nurse it. Drink it slowly. You will get your buzz and not get smashed in the process. This goes for shots too. You don't actually have to down a shot in one gulp. Some of the best shots of whiskey are things you can and should nurse. If you drink too quickly, you will not feel a buzz right away and will be tempted to drink more than you should. When you do that, you will quickly go past slight buzz to full-on drunk, which isn't good.

As the Evening Wears On

Don't ever feel like you have to keep up with other drinkers. Be courageous enough to do your own thing. Once you have had your drink, feel free to switch to water, or a soda or juice, etc. Water will not interfere with your buzz and will help with the dehydration that comes with drinking alcohol.

By this point in the evening, most people will not be able to tell the difference between a glass of water in your hand and a glass of vodka, so they won't notice. And, if they do, they will by and large be respectful and probably envious that you had enough common sense not to overindulge. If they aren't respectful of your drink choices, find a new set of friends.

Be the Designated Driver

If you aren't interested in drinking at all, and if you are of driving age, then you can always offer to be the designated driver. People really do appreciate this, as it allows them to indulge, and it gives you a perfect excuse not to. If people don't accept this particular excuse, then they are engaging in overt peer pressure and you should respond appropriately by calling them on it and finding a new set of friends.

Avoiding Addictions

> *"Happiness is a choice that requires effort at times."*
> - *Anonymous*

There are many types of addictions. People can be addicted to drugs, cigarettes, alcohol, sex, religious cults, collecting cats, and, well, basically anything you can imagine. The word *addiction* carries a negative connotation for a reason. Addicted individuals simply aren't dealing with reality very well. They get lost in whatever they are addicted to, and are never happy. NEVER!

I have no doubt that some people are born with addictive personalities and it doesn't matter what they are exposed to. If a little is good, then a lot must be better. So, they don't just find religion, it consumes their lives. They don't just smoke some marijuana, the pursuit of marijuana consumes their lives. Name the addiction and the metaphor stands. These are the folk that will need professional help to deal with their addictions, as they quite literally can't help themselves.

Make a Choice

For everyone else there is a choice. The best course of action is to not get addicted in the first place. If you know something is addictive, because it says so right on the package, as with cigarettes or alcohol, don't use them.

The same rule goes for drugs. If it is a drug, illegal or prescribed, assume it is addictive. If you don't ever take an illegal drug, then you won't get addicted to it. It is as simple as that. In the case of prescription drugs, take the dose you are supposed to and stop when your doctor tells you to. Then throw out the unused portion so you won't be tempted to take that heavy-duty painkiller for things that simple aspirin can handle. The time to think is before you take an addictive substance. Afterwards is too late.

Becoming Sober

> "Drunkenness is temporary suicide; the happiness that it brings is merely negative, a momentary cessation of unhappiness."
>
> *- Lord Russell*

If you are addicted to something and want to stop, then you have several options. But they all start with a choice. You must choose to end your addiction. If you are to succeed, you will need to make sobriety your priority so that you can continually choose to be sober and not make choices that lead back into addiction. If being sober isn't your priority, then you won't succeed.

Getting Help

Becoming sober is your personal responsibility. No one can do it for you. However, you don't have to go through it alone. Know that there are support groups and professionals out there who can help you. Be sure to find a group and/or professional who actually wants you to get better.

Don't Become Addicted to Recovery

As you can imagine, there is more money to be made by others if you continue to struggle with your addiction instead of getting over it. Additionally, there are many groups that give you props for *trying* to overcome your addiction when the focus should be on *actually overcoming* it. Don't fall into that trap either.

Your goal is to get better, not to try to get better. To paraphrase Master Yoda, "Do or do not, there is no try." When it all comes down to it, the only way to get out of an addiction is to choose not to indulge. As cliché as it seems, you just have to say no.

To Recap

"Prudence must not be expected from a man who is never sober."

- Cicero

Humanists favor allowing individuals to decide for themselves how to pursue happiness, and encourage a legal climate that allows individuals to make their own choices. That doesn't mean, however, that anything goes. You have a choice. You can choose to do things that bring you happiness, or you can choose to do things you know are counterproductive. Say no to things that will cause you and others harm. If you do find yourself battling addiction, take responsibility for your actions, change your behavior, and think before you act so that you can make better choices in the future.

Respect Your elders

"What an elder sees sitting, the young can't see standing."
- Gustave Flaubert

Humanism places an emphasis on education. This is because a good education helps us learn about the world and encourages us to think about our role in it. Plus, the better our understanding is of any given situation, the better our moral reasoning about it will be. And it is through moral reasoning that we can make good decisions that improve our lives and the lives of others. Humanists feel very strongly that education should continue throughout our entire lives.

The problem is that once we get done with our formal education, finding people who can guide us in our continued studies can be difficult. There is no need to worry though as there are plenty of individuals in the world that can help you learn important lessons as you progress though life. Look to anyone who has more experience than you for help. And yes, this does mean that you should be looking to people who are older than you for guidance.

Believe it or not, everyone who is older than you was at one point in time your age. There is a very good chance that whatever it is you are dealing with now, someone older than you has already experienced and learned from it. Working up the nerve to ask someone for a date? Older people have been there and done that. Struggling to cram for a test? Been there, done that. Dealing with the school bully? Been there, done that. Whatever it is you are going through, people who are older than you have gone through it already, and survived!

One of the most important things to realize is that people older than you really do remember what it was like to be your age. I certainly do. This is why people older than you always have that slightly amused look on their faces when you are doing something stupid. They have been there and done that and already learned their lessons.

Learning from the Mistakes Other People Make

"Learn from the mistakes of others. You can't live long enough to make them all yourself."
- Eleanor Roosevelt

Most people eventually do learn from their mistakes. But it is usually a lot less painful to try and learn from other people's mistakes instead of repeating those mistakes yourself.

on't think you are the only person going through whatever it is you are going through. You aren't. It doesn't matter if you are dealing with an abusive parent, the death of a friend, or you are having problems with a really bad crush on someone who isn't paying any attention to you. You aren't the first one to deal with whatever it is you are dealing with.

The Wisdom of Your Elders

All our actions have consequences, and if you have learned what those consequences are, you are in an advantaged position. It doesn't matter that times have changed. Human nature hasn't. When it comes to interpersonal relationships specifically, older people can often have a wealth of information and advice on what to look for and avoid. You would be wise to seek out and heed them. You can save yourself a lot of heartache by listening to and respecting your elders.

If You Want My Advice

> "I have learned silence from the talkative, toleration from the intolerant, and kindness from the unkind; yet, strangely, I am ungrateful to these teachers."
> — Kahlil Gibran

When looking for an older adult from whom to seek advice, it is very important that you look for someone who is first and foremost sane. They should be responsible, compassionate, and ethical. There is no point in seeking out the advice of a person who isn't smart enough to behave properly. Any advice you get from someone who isn't ethical, compassionate, or responsible is of questionable value anyway.

Once you have identified these people, then share with them. When I was a teenager and young adult, I used my mother, my sister, and several of my friends' mothers as advisors. I got good advice on everything from dealing with a date gone psycho and with the emotional after affects of a friend's suicide, to looking for and getting a good job.

It didn't matter what I was going through. They had either dealt with an identical experience personally or had a good friend who had. And, they learned from those experiences and knew what would cause more trouble and what would help. That is why the advice I received from them was almost always the same across the board.

.

Starting Conversations

To get my friend's mothers to give me advice required that I strike up conversations with them. This is very easy to do if you treat the older people around you like real human beings and share with them what is going on in your life. Don't be nervous about seeking out advice from the older people around you. It's your parents' job to provide that advice. If you are seeking the advice of one of your friend's parents, realize that most parents like their children's friends and do like hearing what is going on in their lives.

I honestly can't think of an instance where I got bad advice, so it was well worth the effort of getting to know these women. Plus, I think they really did appreciate that their hard-earned wisdom was being sought and valued by someone. So don't think you are imposing. Most people love to share their wisdom.

Something to Keep in Mind

In order to truly develop a first-class elder advice network, you really do need to respect your elders. People won't bother to give advice to a fool. If you ask for advice and then flagrantly ignore it, your volunteer advisor will quickly learn that there is no point in giving advice to you and won't bother with you in the future. Respect your elders. Learn from your elders and value the advice you receive from your elders by acting on their advice.

Benefits of Respecting Your Elders

> *"It's hard for young players to see the big picture. They just see three or four years down the road."*
> - Kareem Abdul-Jabbar

There are several benefits of having an elder advice network and seeking out the advice of elders throughout your life. Here is what a mentally sane adult can do for you.

- They can put what you are going through into a bigger perspective.
- They can help steer you clear of relationships you should be avoiding.
- They can encourage you in appropriate career choices.
- They can keep you from doing something stupid.
- They can share your triumphs.
- They can help you deal with grief.

As you go through life, your need for an elder advice network does not fade. Yes, you will become more skilled and you will start looking at people younger than you making the same stupid mistakes you did with amusement, and you will be tempted to say things like, "when I was your age..." But never forget that there are still many things you will need to learn and experience, as you get older. Getting married? Getting a divorce? Dealing with the loss of a child, or the loss of a parent? Older people have been there and done that.

Lifelong Learning

> "Some are born with knowledge, some derive it from study, and some acquire it only after a painful realization of their ignorance. But the knowledge being possessed, it comes to the same thing."
>
> - Confucius

"Humanism affirms our ability and responsibility to lead ethical lives of personal fulfillment that aspire to the greater good of humanity."[6] In order to be an ethical person, you must be able to apply moral reasoning to the variety of situations you find yourself in. Unfortunately, moral reasoning is totally dependent on your level of understanding of the situation and your level of understanding is limited by your experiences. Education helps fill in the gaps in your experience so that you can understand things you haven't yet personally experienced.

As you grow older you will find yourself in more and more situations that you may not have any experience with. This is normal. No one is expected to know everything. Smart people seek out the advice of those who have gone before in order to learn what they can before they make really horrid mistakes. You should do the same. And if the person you are seeking advice from is sane as well as ethical, responsible, and compassionate, they can continue to give you great advice on how to cope with the challenges you face, as you get older. In other words, you are never too old to respect your elders and to heed their advice.

---

[6] From *Humanism and its Aspirations,* published by the American Humanist Association in 2003.

Fairy Tale Relationships

"Fairy Tales are more than true; not because they tell us that dragons exist, but because they tell us that dragons can be beaten."

— *G. K. Chesterton*

Judging by the historical record, the subject we humans are most interested in learning about is romance and the sexual relationships that follow. Why else would we have romance and sex manuals going back millennia from all corners of the globe? Because Humanism is concerned with all things human, it is not surprising to find that Humanists are concerned with the quality and character of our relationships. At the heart of our approach we recognize that while we are individuals, we need, enjoy, and find meaning in our relations with others. Humanists seek ethical relationships that are interdependent and equal.

Learning About Love

"Lust is easy. Love is hard. Like is most important."

— *Carl Reiner*

Because all humans are concerned with relationships, detailed books and drawings on how to kiss, have sex, and be in a relationship have been developed and designed in every culture and in every time. People have always looked to literature and the arts to learn about what it means to be in a relationship, how people are supposed to act, and what to expect. Humanists are no exception.

Nowadays, most people are getting their relationship advice from TV shows, movies, and books and, for some people, pornography. This is fine, but only to a point. These are all art forms and while they speak to us about our lives, it is important to remember that they are all forms of fantasy.

Everyone knows that fairy tales aren't real. Yet, the same romantic ideals set forth in fairy tales pervade our modern forms of art and story telling. Just because the formats are more realistic, doesn't mean the stories themselves are. A story is still a form of fantasy.

The problem with learning about relationships from works of fantasy is that you can end up with a distorted view of how things work. The tendency is to expect from yourself and your partners what you see in the fantasy world. Since that often isn't possible or practical, this can lead to feelings of inadequacy, depression, hurt feelings, and discord in the relationship. In short, learning about love from modern-day fairy tales isn't likely to make you happy.

Don't get me wrong; fantasy is a great way to safely imagine how you would behave in different situations. You should keep in mind that it is a fantasy and not reality. While some fantasy is healthy, when it distorts or replaces an individual's sense of reality, it causes trouble. The things you read about and see in books and video usually aren't real. And pornography should not be viewed as a how to manual. More often than not, they do not represent what actually happens in real relationships.

To Put It Simply

The closer your understanding of how you think the world works is to how things really are, the easier the time you will have negotiating the world around you. The easier the time you have negotiating the world around you, the less stress you will have. The less stress you have, the happier you will be. Therefore, one of the best ways to be happy is to embrace reality and recognize the limits of fantasy when learning about relationships.

Truncated Timelines

> *"You have to walk carefully in the beginning of love; the running across fields into your lover's arms can only come later when you're sure they won't laugh if you trip."*
> *- Jonathan Carroll*

The first thing you need to know is that when it comes to telling a romantic story, the courtship must be truncated. In a book, movie, or TV show, the writer needs to get the couple together as quickly as possible to move their story forward. They still need to show that there are sometimes fits and starts to a relationship and perhaps doubts, which is why they rarely get together on the first date. But to move their story forward, they usually need to get the couple together quickly.

This is where the "three date rule" comes from. In film and in books, a couple is usually consummating their fledgling relationship by the third time they have gotten together. Audiences would rarely believe that people would get together on the first or second date, but the need to get the couple together quickly is still there and the third date is about the soonest a couple can consummate their imaginary relationship and still be believable to the audience.

In real life, a courtship between two people can take months and months before a couple decides to date exclusively let alone have sex. Yet, because most people are getting their dating information from movies, it is not surprising to find that in popular culture, many people think that by the third date, if things haven't progressed to an intimate physical level, then it is time to move on. These people were obviously never taught to discern between reality and fantasy.

Basic Dating Rules

> *"I don't understand the whole dating thing. I know right off the bat if I'm interested in someone, and I don't want them to waste their money on me and take me out to eat if I know I'm not interested in that person."*
>
> *- Britney Spears*

Not all parents teach their children a basic set of rules to help them navigate the turbulent waters of relationships. As a result, the number of young people entertaining weird, fantasy-fed ideas about how relationships work is very high, and this causes a lot of unnecessary heartache.

Dating

First, understand that there is a difference between dating and being in a relationship. Dating is about having fun and determining if you are compatible. Just because you like someone and they have agreed to go on a date with you doesn't mean you are in an exclusive relationship with this person. A date is just a date.

While you are dating someone, you should try to limit your physical intimacy to kissing and light petting. Sex is best left to mutually exclusive relationships, which will benefit your health as well as your heart. It is a huge mistake to get intimate with someone because they are available and you haven't really shopped around to find out if they are really right for you or not. The last thing you want to do is have sex with someone who turns out to be crazy or who has other potential serious or dangerous problems.

It takes a minimum of three or four months to determine whether a person you have been dating is crazy or not. Anyone can behave decently and put on a sane face for a short period of time. It is only when you get into the third and fourth months of dating that their true colors start to emerge. This is why older people will tell you time and time again to not rush into an exclusive relationship. Giving yourself plenty of dating time allows you to really find out whether your potential partner is someone you actually want to be with.

Play the Field

Even when you fall head over heels for someone, it is a good idea to give yourself some balance and space by constantly reminding yourself that you are only dating. A good way to do this is by "playing the field." Make sure you are dating at least one other person during the initial stages of dating, especially if you think you have found your heart's true desire. Playing the field in the early stages of dating ensures that when you do select someone to become more intimate with, you are choosing them because you like them the most and that this individual is truly worthy of you.

Playing the field also encourages you to go out and have fun on your dates. Since you aren't expecting to end up in a relationship with everyone you go out with, you free yourself up to accept dates from a wide variety of individuals. If someone seems nice and doesn't seem like they are going to put you in danger or are an axe murderer, go out with them. So what if romance doesn't blossom? At least you will have tested the waters to find out what you really like. And, sometimes, you might be surprised by how someone grows on you.

Not everyone is lucky enough to have their choice of dates. In fact, most of us aren't that lucky. Don't let that stop you or make you feel like you don't have a choice. You do. If you found one person to date you, you can find another. Or, you can choose to stay single and hang out with your friends. It is much better to be single than to be involved with the wrong person or an abusive person. So hold out until you know whether the person you are dating is really worth your time or not.

Exclusive Relationships

Usually, after a few months of dating, it will become obvious whether someone is right for you or not. If they aren't, move on. Usually though, it becomes obvious who your favorite dating partner is and if after four months you have determined that this person has no obvious mental health issues or excessive and potentially dangerous baggage, it is perfectly reasonable to make that dating relationship exclusive.

A decision to make a dating relationship exclusive is something that must be a joint decision between you and your potential partner. It is a decision that must be made explicitly, so that both individuals know where they stand. If your partner does not want to make the relationship exclusive, you can either continue non-exclusive dating or move on and find someone else.

If someone rejects the idea of exclusivity, don't assume they will change their mind. Only continue dating if you are truly content with them seeing other people. If, however, they agree to make the relationship exclusive, congratulations, you are now well on your way to a bona-fide relationship.

To Recap

Because humans find meaning in their relationships, it is important that you approach your relationships as rationally and compassionately as possible. This is the Humanist approach to everything and that includes romance. Don't expect your relationships to be like what you see in the movies or read in a book. Real life doesn't happen like that and if you persist in wanting a fairy tale life, you will be disappointed and unhappy. Date, enjoy yourself, and have fun. Only fools rush in so take your time before committing to an exclusive relationship.

Relationship Advice

"There is only one happiness in life, to love and be loved."
- George Sand

Few people enjoy being single. Most, but not all, would like to find someone that they can spend time with and share life's troubles and triumphs with. Basically we all want someone to love.

Notice here that the emphasis is on someone you can love, not on having someone else be in love with you. Being in love is a wonderful thing. In fact, it is definitely more pleasant to be in love with someone who doesn't return your feelings than it is to have someone love you that you don't feel that way about. Ideally those feelings should be mutual.

Regardless, the rules for relationships haven't changed much since we became human. Sure, different societies encourage and discourage different sorts of relationships for many different reasons. As a matter of public record, Humanists are open to a variety of relationship types, viewing the type of relationship chosen as a matter of personal choice for the individuals involved. As long as relationships are ethical and consensual we don't care what relationships people enter into. And yes, this does mean that we don't care what the gender is of the individuals involved in any given relationship, only that it is ethical and consensual.

That being said, I live in a western society where the norm is heterosexual monogamy so that is the language in which this chapter is written. If you choose homosexual, polyamorous, or polygamous relationships, these principles will still apply. Do a mental translation of the gender terms used to suit your preferences.

Are You the one?

> *"Love is a condition in which the happiness of another person is essential to your own."*
>
> *- Robert Heinlein*

Good relationships are built on mutual respect, affection, and attraction. It is extremely important that you assess whether your potential partner is right for you before you move your relationship forward. You really don't want to get intimate, with all the responsibilities that come with that intimacy, with someone who isn't emotionally healthy or who for whatever reason is incapable of reciprocating your affection and respect.

If you want to be in a healthy relationship, it is equally important that avoid the common traps that emotionally immature people fall into. Many otherwise smart people sabotage what otherwise might be a good relationship because of emotional and manipulative game playing.

How to Tell if You Are in a Healthy Relationship

> *"Lots of people want to ride with you in the limo, but what you want is someone who will take the bus with you when the limo breaks down. "*
>
> *- Oprah Winfrey*

Basically, you are looking for someone who displays all three traits of the true holy trinity. In other words, a healthy relationship is predicated on both parties being compassionate, ethical, and responsible. If one of those traits is missing, there will be trouble in paradise.

When it comes down to it, emotionally healthy people tend to end up in emotionally healthy relationships with other emotionally healthy people. Emotionally sick and damaged people tend to get into emotionally sick and damaged relationships.

With relationships specifically, there are five essential characteristics you should be looking for in a mate. If your potential partner fails in any one of these areas, run for the hills.

The Importance of Being Earnest

In order for a relationship to work, the individuals in it must be serious about being in the relationship. It is perfectly okay to not want to be in a relationship at any given time in your life. In fact, there are many good reasons to avoid serious relationships and concentrate on dating or on being happy by yourself. Getting over a broken heart from a previous relationship is a perfect example.

However, if a relationship is what you seek, you will only succeed if the individual you are contemplating a relationship with is also interested in being in a relationship with you. If all they want to do is date, you can't be in a relationship with them.

Honesty Is the Best Policy

Healthy relationships are based on trust. If you don't trust your partner, you will be very annoying to them, checking up on them and double guessing their actions for hidden meanings and betrayal. If you don't trust your partner, you will be miserable. It is best to avoid relationships with people you don't trust, regardless of how passionately you feel about them. Likewise, if you are not trustworthy, then you will make your partner miserable. Either way, honesty plays an important role in relationships.

You can almost always assess whether your partner is being honest with you during the dating phase. Either they are honest with you about how they are feeling and whether they are or are not dating others. You need to be honest as well. If you aren't earnest about being in a relationship with someone, you need to make that clear at the outset. If you change your mind, you need to make that clear as well. When my husband and I were first dating, we were both sure we didn't want to be in a serious relationship and we were both okay with that. When that changed for him, he told me. And so, I was given the opportunity to consider whether I wanted to be in a relationship with him. It was all very explicit and we never lied to one another about where we were in relationship to one another, and that is why our relationship is a good one.

Keeping how you feel about these things a secret doesn't do anyone any good. The other people in your life have a right to decide for themselves what they can deal with and what they can't. If you are dating multiple people, then they all should know that. If they don't want to be part of your dating pool, that is their choice to make, not yours. It would be selfish of you to prevent them from understanding the playing field they are on by lying to them to spare their feelings.

Limitations on Honesty

Do not kiss and tell. While it is okay to let the various people in your life know that you are dating other people, it is not acceptable to give them details. This means no names, no background information, no talking about what you did on a date with someone else, and definitely no sexual details. It is mean and counterproductive to try and make the various people in your life jealous in that way, and that sort of game playing will make emotionally healthy people run for the hills.

Like Father Like Son

Healthy people have healthy relationships with their parents. Of specific interest to you is the quality and nature of your potential mate's relationship with the parent who is the same gender as you. For girls, this means you want to know if your guy (or gal) likes his mom. Does he respect her? How does he treat her? What lessons has he learned from her? How does he talk about her? Guys, you want to know the same thing about your girl's relationship with her father.

There are two good reasons for paying attention to what your potential mate says about their parents. First, if they have a good relationship with their parents it is a good indication that they are emotionally healthy and are capable of being in a good and healthy relationship with you.

Second, their relationship with their opposite-sex parent tells you everything you need to know about how they feel about the opposite sex. When people like their opposite-sex parent, it means that they probably actually like members of the opposite sex, and this genuine like of the opposite sex translates into healthy relationships.

Good Advice

Do not confuse lust for and attraction to the opposite sex for liking the opposite sex. If a girl hates her father, there is a good chance she hates men in general even if all she thinks about is men all the time. If a man hates his mother, then there is a good chance he hates all women, even though he is seeking out the attention of women. Trust me, you really don't need this sort of hassle.

Boring Is Good

The best advice I ever got was from a girlfriend who told me to find someone boring. Like me, she had been in a weird and abusive relationship with someone who had some sort of emotional trauma going on every two weeks. When she found the man she eventually married, she liked him specifically because he was boring, meaning he wasn't in a continuous state of emotional trauma and drama. One of the things I love about my husband is that when it comes to relationship drama, he is positively boring, meaning he is not experiencing emotional trauma on a daily basis.

Looking for someone who is boring in an emotional health context doesn't mean that you find a dull, drab, uninteresting person. It simply means that you don't want someone who is a drama king or queen. Emotionally healthy people don't have that much drama going on in their lives. Don't get me wrong, healthy people have the same challenges everyone else has, but they don't make mountains out of molehills. They simply deal with their problems and move on. They don't feel the need to involve everyone within earshot. If you have ever dated a drama king or queen you will understand that dating someone who is emotionally healthy and doesn't break down when something minor happens in their lives is quite boring in comparison, but boring in a really good way.

Compatible Problem Solving Skills

Which brings us to the final and most important aspect of healthy relationships: having compatible problem solving skills. Because people in relationships become partners in dealing with life's problems, it is important that their problem-solving skills are compatible. Incompatible approaches lead to unnecessary conflict during routine problem solving. For instance, what are you going to do for lunch or dinner? It is a simple enough question and quite routine for a couple living together. Yet, there are many couples for which finding an answer to this question involves a struggle that is so passionately waged that they yell and fight about it. And, it never gets any better.

They simply don't deal with basic problem solving the same way, and they haven't figured out how to reconcile their different approaches. So they end up yelling and fighting every night. And not just about dinner, but about everything.

Though this might work for some, it would be nicer if you didn't have that sort of drama over mundane things. So look for someone who solves problems the same way you do. When you are tested and need to work together as a team, do you simply solve the problem and move on or not? This is why traveling together with someone, canoeing, or doing something else that requires teamwork is such a good way to test compatibility. When you are forced to work together, you will find out very quickly if your problem-solving skills are compatible or not. If not think hard about whether you want to continue on in a relationship with this person.

For Example

My first date with my husband forced us into a Plan D for dinner. Our first three attempts to get food failed—restaurants weren't open, lines were too long, and we wouldn't make our movie on time. Eventually we ate at a fast-food restaurant. The important thing was that neither of us were the slightest bit concerned about the changes we had to make to our plans. We both rolled with it. One option was closed down, we discussed the next plan, and when that fell through we discussed the next plan, until we found one that worked. I knew right away we had compatible problem-solving skills. This was only reinforced on our second date when we went canoeing and spent the entire day singing songs together. The friends we went with spent their day arguing. Not surprisingly, I am now happily married to my husband and my friend's relationship ended in a rather ugly mess.

To Recap

If you want to be in a healthy relationship, you need to look for someone who is emotionally healthy. You also need to hold up your end of the relationship. You want someone who is able to cope with life's problems, likes their parents, is honest, doesn't get upset easily, and who has the same problem-solving skills as you do. And then, you need to be worthy of them by cultivating the traits of the true holy trinity in yourself by being ethical, compassionate, and responsible.

Run for the Hills

*"It's important to have toxic people out of our lives, so that
we can be fully available to the good people who need us."*
                                                    - J. E. Brown

While we Humanists would like it if every person we met was ethical,
compassionate, responsible, and would work together with us in peace and
harmony, we aren't stupid. We do live in the real world. The reality is, no matter
how much we might want them to be; some people aren't all that nice.
Unfortunately, people don't come with warning signs, and staying away from bad
people can take a lot of courage.

There are some people who you are better off avoiding. These are the people who
are harmful for you to be around. While these people can come from any aspect of
your life—acquaintances, co-workers, relatives and so-called friends—such
people are particular toxic when they are your romantic interest. Once you
identify a person as someone you should avoid, run for the hills and get as far
away as possible. Don't stick around to see how it turns out and don't give that
person continued access to you unless ordered to by a court. If you perceive
danger, don't second-guess yourself. If a red flag goes off in your head, then there
is a problem. You aren't just imagining it. Sticking it out to see if your concerns
manifest themselves is a lot like rubbernecking at the scene of the accident, except
for one thing: you are in the car that is about to crash. Better to get out while you
still can.

This advice can be hard to take if you find yourself in love with someone who is
bad for you. It isn't your fault. It can and does happen to almost everyone at some
point. Don't make the mistake of thinking that the person you are in love with
now is the only person you will ever love. It doesn't matter how passionate your
love is. If they are bad for you, you need to look elsewhere. There really are a lot
of fish in the sea and the more time you waste on inappropriate and/or harmful
people, the less time you will be spending on people who will make your life a
joyful and happy experience. Really. I have been there and done that and know
what I am talking about.

Sanity Is Totally Underrated

People giving advise about relationships rarely mention the single most important
aspect of someone's personality that you should look for: sanity. For the purposes
of this discussion, people who are "insane" don't just have a few "issues." Rather,
they have pathological problems that prevent them from dealing with other people
productively and rationally.

It is simply impossible to have a sane and healthy relationship with someone who isn't sane. This isn't to say you can't have a happy relationship with someone who has some problems. It is only that being in a relationship with someone who has a few "issues" requires more work and a strong commitment to deal with the bad times, which will occur, as a matter of course, more often than they do in a sane and healthy relationship. On the other hand, being involved with someone who is totally incapable of dealing with other people rationally is not something you can work through.

Being sane has nothing to do with intelligence. There are some very smart people who are totally insane and some people who think more slowly than the average person, who have more common sense in them than I do. Sanity is also unrelated to the level of relationship baggage a person might be carrying. Everyone has some baggage. It is how you deal with that baggage that determines whether you are sane or not.

Relationships to Avoid

> "I just broke up with someone and the last thing she said to
> me was 'You'll never find anyone like me again!' I'm thinking,
> 'I should hope not! If I don't want you, why would I want
> someone like you?"
>
> *- Anonymous*

What follows are some examples of mild to moderate forms of insanity, otherwise known as people who are incapable of behaving rationally in a relationship. If you are with someone exhibiting these symptoms, run for the hills and get as far away from them as possible.

Drama Queens and Kings

People who are emotionally damaged tend to have weekly or biweekly dramas that they launch into. Whether it is that their bike got stolen or they scratched some furniture or they need to go into detox, it doesn't matter. Drama queens and kings always have something wrong going on and that something is apparently more than they can handle emotionally. These episodes also serve as handy excuses as to why they aren't behaving in a responsible, rational, or reliable way. Weekly or biweekly episodes are a sign that you are dealing with a sick and damaged person.

Drama queens and kings are counting on the fact that normal and healthy people are compassionate. Here is how the typical drama plays out. They have a problem and you, as a compassionate and responsible person, try to reassure them, calm them down, and help them solve their problem *du jour*. And, you succeed. Then, a week later, something else happens and you have to do it all over again.

What you need to understand is that it is never going to get better. If they are prone to frequent dramatic episodes, even if the drama is about something new each week and regardless of how real the problem is, you will have to deal with these episodes as long as you are involved with the person. That isn't a happy prospect. It is emotionally draining to be with this sort of person. Drama queens and kings will wear you down and make your life miserable if you stay with them.

Don't worry about leaving them and running for the hills. They will be okay as soon as they find their next potential victim ... I mean romantic relationship on which to practice their drama skills. And because they really do need an audience for their dramas, don't be surprised if they replace you within a couple of weeks.

First Date Confessions

As a general rule, most people will tell you exactly what is wrong with them on the first date; so pay attention to what your date tells you. Use your first date to ask questions to see how your date feels about his or her parents, what he or she is looking for in a relationship, and why previous relationships ended.

Most people know what is wrong with themselves, and if they are really struggling, then their personal struggles will be their favorite topic of conversation. Addictive personalities will love to tell you all about how they overcame their cocaine/alcohol/whatever addiction. Obsessive-compulsives will tell you stories about how their last lover didn't clean the soap bubbles off the bar of soap after washing their hands. People who hate their parents will tell you all about how horrible their parents are. Take all of these issues seriously. If your date tells you something that raises a red flag, don't go on a second date with them, no matter how cute and earnest they appear to be.

Bad Boys and Poison Women

People who exude a tremendous amount of animal/sexual magnetism are to be avoided at all costs. That high level of sexual energy and magnetism is most likely hiding a nasty, narcissistic personality that you really don't want to be around for any length of time.

Bad boys and poison women are amongst the hardest people to avoid. They are, after all, magnetic. They want us, and we love the fact that they want us. It makes us feel good and sexy and virile. However, while they exude a promise of wild and passionate sex, these people engage in sex in a very selfish way.

Believe it or not, as important as sexual attraction is in a relationship, there is more to life than sex. Healthy relationships are based on a well-rounded attraction to the other person. Because hollow sex is all that bad boys and poison women have to offer to a relationship, at some point, either they will leave you for another sexual toy, or you will realize how uncomfortably insane they are and move on to a more balanced and healthy relationship. Either way, these are short-term relationships at best.

It can be very tempting to indulge in a little meaningless sex with this sort of person. It can make you feel very mature to engage in an approach to sex that is so open and unfettered with old-fashioned morals. Don't fall into that trap. It isn't mature and those old-fashioned morals serve a good purpose. The reason these sexual magnets should be avoided at all costs is two-fold. First, they are probably carriers of a variety of sexually transmitted diseases because they probably have had a lot of reckless unprotected sex with a lot of different people. You really don't need to be picking up a potentially fatal disease just to satisfy a sexual desire. The other reason to avoid them is because they are also insane narcissists. Giving an insane narcissist access to you is always dangerous. You never know what they might be capable of during or after the relationship.

Basic Maintenance

People who cannot seem to take care of basic details in their lives are trouble. Most people are able to get and hold onto a job, even if it is a job they don't particularly like. Sane people take care to make sure they have housing, transportation, food, and other necessities. Sane people also keep themselves clean by taking showers regularly and brushing their teeth. If you are with someone who has trouble with any or all of these areas of basic life maintenance, cut them loose and run for the hills.

It is perfectly acceptable and expected that a partner in a long-term, healthy relationship will help pick up the slack for their partner when things get tough. However, that is predicated on the expectation that these problems are temporary and not habitual. If, when you first start out in a relationship someone is asking for this sort of help, it should raise a humungous red flag.

The problem with people who start off a relationship with a whole list of problems that need solving isn't that they have had a run of hard luck, or aren't making enough money. The problem is that they aren't capable of managing the basics of life. What these sorts of people are looking for is a knight in shining armor to take care of them. As with the drama queens and kings, this is emotionally and financially draining. Regardless of how financially well off you might be, these people cannot be helped. People who lack basic maintenance skills are so problematic that even sugar daddies and sugar mamas give them wide berth.

Don't worry about leaving people who lack basic skills high and dry. Like the drama queens and kings, they are preying on compassionate, responsible people. When you leave, they will look for and find someone else to help sort out their lives pretty quickly.

<u>For Example</u>
I had a friend who for years was having landlord trouble. For six years she told me how she needed to find a new place to live. Yet, when she was finally evicted, it came as a complete surprise to her and she had no alternative housing arranged. Nor had she saved any money for a deposit on a new place. It took her all of one day to find a guy to take her in and "help her get back on her feet." The last time I talked to her, she was still struggling with her housing issues. Several years after being evicted she was still relying on the kindness of others for her housing requirements. Don't get emotionally involved with someone like this. Just don't.

Fools Rush In

If you find yourself in a new dating relationship and your partner is pushing for a full-fledged emotional commitment right away, then you should probably run for the hills.

Emotionally healthy people allow themselves time to get to know their dating partners before deciding whether or not they want to get involved more intimately. People who push for a full commitment early on because they are passionately in love with you have something wrong with them.

Don't allow yourself to be pushed too quickly. Yes, it is flattering and easy to get caught up in their passion and excitement. The problem is that anyone can be charming and pretend to be sane for three or four months. Until you know whether the person you are dating is emotionally stable, don't make any long-term commitments and don't have sex with them. People who rush things are usually incredibly insecure and that isn't just annoying, it also indicates a strong likelihood that they are insane and are hoping you will commit to them before figuring it out. Trust me on this one, you do not want to be in a relationship with someone who is incredibly insecure and you really do not want to be having sex with someone who will react irrationally and/or erratically if and when you decide to end the relationship.

For Example
Having had to get a restraining order against an insane ex-boyfriend turned stalker, I can say with some authority that you don't want to risk having a love child with someone until you have assured yourself that they are not going to harm you physically or emotionally. As a result of the time I spent in my local clerk of the courts office dealing with my situation, I saw far too many women forced into legal relationships with abusive men simply because they had had a child with the guy. Don't be one of them. And men, you do not want to be forced into a legal relationship with a crazy woman because of a love child either. So think before you commit.

Exceeding Your Minutes

Another warning sign to look for is excessive phone use. People who are excessively insecure will call you all the time. They will send you emails at all hours of the day and night. It may seem romantic that they are thinking of you all the time and writing you romantic poetry at 3 a.m., but in reality, it should be sending up red flags.

The problem is that normal people have lives. Normal people don't have time to be on the phone ten times a day. Normal people are usually sleeping at 3 a.m. and so won't be on the computer to email you. Normal people don't have four hours to spend on the phone every night. If someone is calling you and emailing you all the time to tell you they are thinking about you and sending you the latest poem you have inspired, be afraid. Be very afraid.

These people are not only insecure, they are obsessive and controlling and probably abusive. In fact, one of the first signs that you are dealing with a controlling and abusive personality is excessive phone calling. What they are really doing is checking up on you to make sure you are where you said you would be. Excessive phone calls aren't romantic. They are scary and frightening. Run for the hills and get away as quickly and as safely as possible.

Anger Management Issues/Abuse

It should go without saying that if you find yourself dealing with an abusive person; you should run for the hills. Unfortunately, it isn't always that clear cut. Many of the early signs of an abusive personality are not that obvious. On top of that, abusive individuals also are incredibly good at manipulating emotions, thus making it very difficult to extract your self once involved. However, once you realize you are dealing with an abusive person, you should get out as quickly and as safely as possible.

How do you tell if your romantic partner is abusive? Well, are they angry a lot? Do they blow up easily and then apologize for it? Do they become emotionally traumatized at the slightest thing? Normal people don't get upset that easily. So, if you are with someone who is angry or upset a lot, get out as soon as possible.

Another way to tell you are dealing with an abusive individual is whether they are not they attempt to control your life. This could be as simple as pouting whenever they don't get their way, in order to manipulate you into doing their bidding. Or it could be more drastic, like throwing away your phone book so that you can no longer contact your friends. It isn't unusual for controlling people to try and limit your access to other people and friends. If you have a good support network around you, it makes it more difficult for anyone to control you. If someone seeks to limit your other friendships, run for the hills.

If your partner tries to monopolize all your time and does not like it when you go places without them. If when you do go out and do something without them, they let you know how upset it makes them, have a tantrum, and then check on you when you are out, know that you are dealing with a controlling person. Run away as quickly as possible.

If you are insulted, run for the hills. You should never tolerate insults, regardless of how mild that insult might be. Insults are a form of control and you need to consider insults abusive. A slight comment about your posture, weight, singing voice, intelligence, or other aspect of who you are is inappropriate and done to hurt your feelings, and can have dramatically negative impacts on your self esteem. It is abusive and you should not tolerate such behavior from anyone. Which means, if you experience such treatment, the offending individual has relinquished any rights to have contact with you. In other words, run for the hills.

Physical violence is the most obvious form of abuse and again, should not be tolerated. The only way to stop it is to leave as quickly and as safely as possible.

For Happiness' and Safety's Sake

> *"Happiness is nothing more than good health and a bad memory."*
>
> *- Albert Schweitzer*

Humanists seek out healthy, respectful, and ethical relationships. It should go without saying that in order to be in a healthy relationship, you need to avoid unhealthy people. Unfortunately, some people are so emotionally messed up that they are toxic and shouldn't be dated for even small periods of time. These people are mentally unstable, lack the ability for deep emotional commitment, have problems managing their day to day lives, are narcissistically self-centered, and are probably abusive. If you find that you are dating someone who falls into one or all of these categories, run for the hills and don't look back. Your happiness might not be the only thing you are putting at risk.

Breaking Up Is Hard to Do

"Don't cry for a man who's left you, the next one may fall for your smile."

- Mae West

Into each of our lives, a little rain must fall. Ok, it is cliché, but the reality is, unless you are super-duper, unbelievably lucky, you are going to have your heart broken at some point and will most likely break someone else's heart as well. Which is worse, I am not sure.

It is important to understand that this happens to everyone at some point. You will get past it eventually. Plenty of people are able to break up, mend their broken hearts and go on to live healthy productive lives. Many eventually find someone compatible to share their lives with. I am living proof of that.

As a Humanist, what you want to strive for is ending your relationships in the same ethical, responsible, and compassionate way you would expect of yourself in other areas of your life. It isn't always easy, but you will feel much better about yourself if you stick to your moral values than if you lapse in a moment of anguish.

Learn the Ropes Before You Have Sex

While Humanists hold no prohibitions on premarital sex, it is a good idea to learn the ins and outs of relationships and specifically how to deal with a broken heart before you introduce sex into your relationships. Trust me, breaking up is hard enough on your heart as it is. Sex only complicates the matter further (more on this in the next chapter). Once you have experienced the good and the bad in relationships, you will be in a much better position to judge whether you want to take on the responsibilities that come with sex. Ditto for moving in together. If you think breaking up is hard to do, try breaking up with someone you are living with.

Basic Break-up Ethics

"I refuse to let what happened to me make me bitter. I still completely believe in love and I'm open to anything that will happen to me."

- Nicole Kidman

When relationships end, regardless of who instigated the break up, you should strive to behave decently, ethically, and responsibly.

Heart Breakers and Heartbroken

Sometimes you will be the heart breaker and sometimes you will have your heart broken. Sometimes, you will be both. Each role has its own responsibilities to ensure that the breakup is as painless as possible. Realize that the people you are breaking up with won't always be as ethical or rational as you, but don't let that stop you from trying to do the right thing.

Advice to the Heart Breaker

If you are the one instigating the break up, do so as honestly and compassionately as possible. Let them know you no longer want to date them or be in a relationship with them. You don't need to give them details on why unless it has to do with you and not anything with them. It is sufficient to simply say this relationship isn't right for you, and then exit gracefully. Don't tell them that you still want to be friends, as that is insulting. Don't return their phone calls for at least a year and don't respond to their emails or try to be nice to them and let them down easy. There is no easy way to break up with someone. The sooner the person you are breaking up with gets over the habit of being able to talk to you and finds someone else to communicate with, the sooner their heart will heal. Being nice by keeping in touch with a person whose heart you have broken only prolongs their agony.

Friendships are only possible after breakups in the rarest of circumstances, and usually only after a few years have passed and both individuals have moved on to other, more successful relationships, so don't hold onto the hope that you could still have this person in your life. To do so would be very selfish of you. Allow the other person to move on.

Advice to the Heartbroken

If you are the one who has been told that your relationship is over, accept this as fact. As much as you might want to argue or convince the other person that the relationship is worth saving, the reality is that it isn't because the other person has decided it isn't. The sooner you accept this as fact, the sooner you can hurt and then heal. Trying to cling to something that once was is painful for both parties and only prolongs the inevitable.

Don't try to be friends with the person, don't call them, and don't write them. You will probably want to, but, if you do call them or write to them or send emails to them, you are only prolonging the habit of having regular contact with them. You need to break that habit and find new outlets for your energy. In fact, the only contact you should have after a breakup really is to exchange the stuff you have that belongs to the other person. Don't try to give back any of the presents they gave you. If you no longer want that necklace or golf bag, give it away to charity. If you try to give it back, it will most likely be refused. The only exception to this rule is if the gift was a family heirloom. If you received a family heirloom the nice thing to do is offer to return it so that it can stay within the family.

This Doesn't Feel Right

You will mostly likely be going through various stages of grief when your relationships end. So expect to experience a wide variety of emotions. The important thing to remember is that you don't have to act on your emotions. In fact, when mending a broken heart, it is better if you don't act. It is perfectly acceptable to feel the feeling and not act on it.

This is because during a breakup emotions are often quite strong. You may feel anger and the desire for revenge. You are going to need to put extra effort into thinking rationally so that you don't let your emotions run away with you. This is all about doing what you know is right, even if your heart is telling you to do something completely different.

If you feel like you want to yell at your ex and tell them how you feel about how horrible a person they are, go ahead and write it down, yell into your pillow, punch a pillow or tell your pet fish how horrible that person was. What you don't want to do is contact your ex to tell them personally. Write them a nasty letter if you want to, but don't mail it. Sometimes it is very helpful to put together a breakup box as a ritual to clear the remnants of that relationship out of your life. Think twice about whether you really want to get rid of the things you are putting in it, and don't send that box to your ex. Toss it out or give it to charity. Again, if you have an heirloom that belongs to the other person, offer to give it back to them.

The point is, find productive outlets for your emotions and think before you act so that you don't end up doing something you will regret later.

Getting Out of the Habit

A lot of what happens emotionally during a break up has to do with habit. You are in the habit of talking to this person all the time, and then you break up and no longer have them to talk to. You are in the habit of getting hugs whenever you need one, and suddenly that comfort is no longer there. You get the idea. Getting over someone is all about finding new outlets for your basic interpersonal needs and breaking the habits you got into with your ex.

It is not unusual to have trouble not calling, emailing, or otherwise contacting your ex regardless of how crappy you feel afterward. The brain is incredibly good at rationalizing the things it wants to do, regardless of how stupid doing so might be. This is especially true when you are trying to break a habit, which is why habits are so hard to break. You have to power through those urges and not do what you really do know is wrong. If you really are having strong urges to call or email your ex, post stickers to your phone, computer, and wherever else they are needed asking yourself this very important question: "Do you really want to call pain?" This will help you think before you pick up the phone. If you resist temptation, it should only take a month or so before you no longer have such inappropriate urges. Be strong. If you give in to your urges, you have to start all over again and it will take that much longer for your heart to heal.

Physical Needs

One of the hardest parts about breaking up is that your physical needs are no longer being met. And no, I am not talking about sex. When we are in a relationship, we hold hands, we hug, we kiss, we snuggle, and all of that is wonderful and helps us maintain proper mental health. We humans are social animals after all. When we aren't in a relationship, we get that petting from our friends and family members. When we are in a relationship, we get it almost exclusively from our partners.

So, when you break up, be aware that unless you find a replacement for this everyday sort of physical contact, you will suffer. This is why having a strong and reliable set of friends is so important. Don't be afraid to ask your friends for hugs after a breakup. Shoulders to cry on also work, but only for a short period of time. Your goal is to regain your sense of happiness without your ex in your life. Get out and about and mix with other people. It is hard to be depressed when you are out with a group of people having fun. It isn't impossible, but the key is not to try to have fun, but to simply enjoy the presence of other people.

Advice to Friends of the Heartbroken

Being there for your friends does indeed mean listening to them and, most importantly, providing them with the positive physical reinforcement that a hug represents. Also be aware that sometimes the best thing you can do for a heartbroken friend is to tell them a joke and get them laughing again. Don't ignore their need to talk about the ex, but introducing humor, especially humor unrelated to the ex and relationships in general, is a good way to gently encourage them to talk about other things and find joy in life again.

What you don't want to do is bring up the subject when your friend is ready to move on. A simple "how are you" is an open-ended question. If your friend wants to talk about the breakup, they will; if they don't, they won't. If they don't go there, you don't go there. There is simply nothing more annoying and exhausting than having to relive a painful breakup simply because your friends and family don't feel they are being truly supportive of you unless they get you to cry on their shoulders. Be a true friend, not a self-centered one. Let your friend decide when and if to talk about their broken heart.

Rebounds and Finding Someone New

There is a truism about breakups, and that is, whoever finds a new lover first, is usually the most miserable. So, if you break up with someone and you find out that you were replaced in short order, don't be upset and hurt, realize that your ex really is a miserable person and that you are better off without them.

Your goal should be to find your balance again as an individual. That means as a solo person. If you aren't happy being alone, then you won't be happy in a relationship. Take the time after a breakup to rediscover yourself and the things that make you happy. There is no rush to find someone new unless you are totally insecure. In which case, you are probably a miserable person who will never find true happiness. If you do want to find true happiness, find it in yourself.

One of the reasons people rush into new relationships is because they miss the contact, both physical and mental, that a relationship provides. Again, if you have a strong network of friends, this won't be an issue for you. If you don't have a strong network of friends, go out and create one. This is about the most important thing you can do for yourself after a breakup.

The main problem with rebound relationships is that they are not able to stand on their own and so are inevitably temporary. Rebound relationships are entirely defined by how they are not like the previous relationship, or as a replacement for the previous relationship. Again, that relationship is over and the sooner you realize it, the sooner you can move on. Rebounds are just a way of trying to avoid the inevitable.

Dating After a Breaking Up

I am not saying don't date. If you really are having trouble disentangling from a previous relationship, going out on a date with someone new might be the thing you need to stop yourself from calling the ex and opening your eyes to all the possibilities out there. Dating is also a nice reminder that there really are other fish in the sea. Don't attempt to force any of your dates into a relationship. Dating is about all you will want to take on while you are recovering from a broken heart. Relationships are out of the question.

If you meet someone you think might have potential for the future, keep in touch with him or her, but don't start dating him or her until you feel like you can judge a prospective partner on his or her own merits and not as a contrast to what happened in your previous relationship. Breakups done properly don't take more than a few months, and most of your prospects will still be on the market in that time. And, if they aren't, there are plenty of other fish in the sea.

If you find yourself dating someone who is recently heartbroken, date them only if they are fun to go out with, but resist being pulled into a full-fledged relationship with them until or unless they are truly recovered. If you rush in with them you will quickly find out what it is like to be the rebound relationship. Always being compared to their ex, and then being dumped when they finally come to their senses and start looking for someone more permanent and without the baggage they placed on you.

A Word About Getting Out of an Abusive Relationship

> "No man is worth your tears and the one that is won't make you cry."
>
> — *Brian Littrell*

If you find yourself in a relationship with an abusive person and have decided to get out, be smart about how you go about it. Trust your instincts. In general, if the abuse is mostly verbal and your partner doesn't have a cache of weapons and doesn't enjoy watching violent movies, then you can probably end it and then deal with a bit of stalking and continued attempts to manipulate you until they finally give up and leave you alone. You might decide you need a restraining order to help you with this phase, but don't expect it to work too well. If you do get one, it will at least give you some ability to call upon law enforcement to help you keep your ex away from you, and perhaps give you a good reason why not to get in touch with your manipulative ex (and for those of you who have never been in an abusive relationship, yes, that is a problem). Keep in mind that abusive people aren't just males. Females can also be abusive. Regardless of the gender of your abuser, trust your instincts.

If, however, your soon-to-be ex has violent tendencies, you are going to need a lot more help and it would be a good idea to hide your trail when you leave to make it as impossible as possible to find you. Only you can judge how your ex will respond to a restraining order and, again, trust your instincts. The number of women who have been killed the day their abusive partners received their restraining orders is legend. Restraining orders aren't for everyone. If you think your partner will blow up and try to hurt you if you leave, then he probably will. In order to get out safely, you will need to have a plan and help to implement it, and you will need to assemble that plan on the sly so that your abuser doesn't suspect anything until your plan is sprung. Then, you will need to stick to your plan.

Getting Help

You are going to need friends you can trust to get out of an abusive relationship. These friends will help shield you and hide you from your abuser when you leave and will help keep you from returning to that abusive relationship after you have gotten out, but only if you don't lie to your friends. And yes, that is an issue. Because of how manipulative an abuser is, your resolve to get out of the relationship will be tested on a nearly constant basis. You won't make the decision once and be done with it. You will need to make it again and again and again. Stay firm.

Everything a normal person experiences during a break up is more intense and severe when breaking up with an abuser. This is because abusers are incredibly manipulative and all the emotions of the relationship have been heightened as a matter of course. The main reason to trust your friends and not your own head when exiting an abusive relationship is that being a victim of abuse, even if it is only verbal abuse, distorts your sense of what is appropriate behavior and what isn't. Really.

For Example

When I left an emotional abuser turned stalker, I was in complete denial I was being stalked, even though I was planning to go into hiding when the guy came to town by staying with a friend he didn't know in another city. I really didn't believe I was being stalked though it was obvious to everyone else. Fortunately, the people around me recognized the severity of what was happening and eventually got me to recognize that reality too. It took a few months, but I finally got it. In one instance a friend had handed me information about my state's stalking laws with the phone number of the clerk of the court's phone number to report what was happening to me. I told them I didn't need it. They nodded knowingly and told me to hold onto that information, just in case. I eventually ended up using that information.

Another example of how skewed your perspective can become as a result of abuse was when my stalker reduced his daily calling to only a few calls a day, as opposed to the sixty or seventy calls a day he had been making every day for the past year. I told the FBI agent dealing with my case that he could drop it and work on something more important. He asked me if I understood that three calls a day were still too many calls, especially since the relationship had ended two years previously. The truth was, I didn't know that it was still a problem. I truly felt like I could deal with three calls a day. It was such an improvement over what had been happening. Now, in hindsight, I realize how ridiculous my perspective must have seemed to the agent. If you have been in an abusive relationship, your judgment on what constitutes appropriate behavior can't be trusted, so rely on the judgment of your friends and family members and the various legal professionals you are dealing with instead.

Finding Happiness Again

> *"Don't cry because it's over. Smile because it happened."*
> *- Dr Seuss*

As I said at the beginning, at some point, unless you are unusually lucky, you will experience the breakup of a relationship. The quickest way to finding your happiness again is to remember to be ethical, honest, compassionate, and responsible during this period regardless of what else happens or what the other person does. Being happy the Humanist way means being able to look at yourself in the mirror and know you behaved like a decent civilized person despite it all. Take care of yourself and your needs. Don't rush into anything new, and above all else avoid falling back into old habits with your ex.

Things Your Mother Never Told You About Sex

"I don't know the question, but sex is definitely the answer"
- Woody Allen

Sex is considered one of the most fundamental topics we humans ever discuss. Everyone is concerned with it, we want it, we want to do it well, and we want to assure ourselves of our own virility in regards to it. In 1976, the American Humanist Association published a Sexual Bill of Rights and Responsibilities.[7] The purpose of this document was "to enhance the quality of sexuality by emphasizing its contributions to a significant life," and that "human beings should have the right to express their sexual desires and enter into relationships as they see fit, as long as they do not harm others or interfere with their rights to sexual expression." "This new sense of freedom, however, should be accompanied by a sense of ethical responsibility."

First Things First

"Don't knock masturbation - it's sex with someone I love"
- Woody Allen

Let's be clear: if it involves two or more people and one or more sets of genitalia, it counts as sex. For you younger folk, that does indeed mean that oral sex and mutual masturbation qualify as sex in addition to various penetration schemes. Solo masturbation is not included in this definition, as it is a private matter and not only does everyone do it, it is good for your mental health.

The first thing you need to know is that sex between partners does not a relationship make. Just because you have sex with someone doesn't mean you are in a relationship with them. You are only in a relationship with someone if you have both agreed to date each other exclusively. It has nothing to do with sex. That is not to say that sex can't be a nice addition to a relationship, but it is not what defines a relationship.

---

[7] Full text of the Humanist Bill of Sexual Rights and Responsibilities can be found on the American Humanist Association website at http://www.americanhumanist.org/about/sexual-rights.html

A Good Rule of Thumb

"Vibrators? I think they are great. They keep you out of stupid sex."

- Anne Heche

Contrary to how it is portrayed in the movies, sex doesn't just happen in real life. Yes, you can get swept up in a passionate moment, but it is only a moment. Unless you have a brain disorder, your brain doesn't stop working and thinking. It is never inappropriate to take a short break from the passion to consider what you are about to do and whether you really want to do it, and if you do, where the heck is that condom!?!

Taking a short thinking break isn't going to stop the sex from happening if it is something you both want to do. A good rule of thumb is that if you want to have sex with someone new, don't. Wait a day and see if you still feel that way tomorrow. Entering into a sexual relationship comes with responsibilities and it is best to enter into those responsibilities with your eyes wide open and with the lights on.

Advice to Women

Do not have sex with a guy as a way to get into a relationship with him. It won't work. If a guy is pressuring you to have sex, it is not because he likes you as a person. It is because he wants to have sex and he is hoping you will oblige. If he stops dating you because you didn't want to have sex with him on the third date, good riddance! He wasn't the sort of person who will make you happy anyway. Men who pressure women to have sex early on in a relationship are usually unfaithful. So, unless you want that sort of heartache in your life, let the loser leave.

Men who like you will want to spend time with you regardless of whether you are having sex with them or not. These are the sort of men you should be looking for.

Advice to Men

In case you weren't aware of this already, women who have sex with you are expecting to be in a relationship with you as a result of their sexual favors. If you don't want to be in a relationship with them, don't have sex with them. If a woman tells you that a one-night stand is okay and that she isn't expecting anything further from you, don't believe her. She really is hoping to lure you into a relationship, whether she knows it or not.

The question you need to ask yourself is this; do you really want to have sex with someone who might turn out to be crazy and vindictive? If not, keep your pants on and wait until you know whether they are emotionally stable or not.

Advice to Teens

While your bodies and hormones are raging and your desire for sex is increasing, you should actually try to refrain from sex entirely until you are older. There are very good reasons why the adults around you almost unanimously agree that young people should wait until they are emotionally more mature to engage in sex.

Relationships are tough, especially for young people learning to navigate their way through them. You need to experience dating first to learn how to date, how to be in romantic relationships, and all that follows. This is a learning process that will last a lifetime. The heartaches that come with the eventual breakups at this age are hard enough to deal with emotionally without introducing sex into the mix. Sex makes an already hard to deal with emotional experience that much harder and unnecessarily more painful.

Take the time when you are young to learn the ropes of relationships before introducing sex into the mix. No one who truly likes you is going to break up with you for not having sex. And, anybody who does isn't someone you want to be with anyway. This rule applies for anyone of any age (not just young people).

Once you know what the consequences are of relationships good and bad (and notice the plural, *relationships*), then you will be in a much better place to handle the emotional consequences of adding sex to a relationship.

It is also helpful to learn how to recognize a good, healthy relationship and bad, unhealthy ones before engaging in sex. Trust me on this; you do not want to have sex with someone who is bad for you or, worse, someone who is emotionally or mentally unstable. You really don't want to go there. The only way to know the difference is to experience them. And, until you can tell the difference between good relationships and bad ones, you really should not be having sex.

The Costs and Consequences of Sex

"Sex always has consequences. When Hitler's mother spread her legs that night, she effectively canceled out the spreading of fifteen to twenty million other pairs of legs."
- George Carlin

Everything has a cost. Before you act, you really need to consider whether you can handle the consequences. And this is doubly true when it comes to sex. Anyone who tells you that sex is no big deal is either lying or isn't doing it right. Sex is a big deal and it has emotional, physical, and sometimes financial consequences. Before you have sex with someone, make sure you are prepared for those consequences. This is where being responsible comes into play.

Your Heart

First and foremost is your heart. If you are having sex for the wrong reasons, you will regret it afterward, and that kind of ruins the experience. Sex is best when it is a loving expression of your feelings for another person. When you are sharing a part of yourself in a very intimate way with someone you love, it can be magical. If, however, you are having sex to keep your partner with you, then when (not if) they leave you, you will be miserable. The question you need to ask yourself is, if the worst that could happen happens and this person never calls you again, how will you feel about what you have done?

Your Health

Having sex with the wrong individual can kill you. Sexual transmitted diseases (STDs) are real, and if you have sex, you are at risk of contracting one. You can mitigate that risk by choosing your sexual partners very carefully, making sure that you are only having sex in mutually exclusive relationships, making sure each partner is tested for STDs before engaging in sex, and using protection anyway. If you think all this would kill the moment, consider how bad it would be if it actually killed you instead.

Sex can obviously lead to pregnancy, even if you use precautions. And if you aren't prepared for that possibility, you might want to hold off on having sex until and unless you are ready to handle an unintended pregnancy. Also, if you don't think your partner can handle that consequence, don't have sex with him or her.

Finally, there are sometimes financial consequences. Sex with prostitutes isn't the only sort of sex that costs money. Having a child, even if you give it away, costs money. Contracting an STD costs money. Affairs can be very expensive. People have lost their jobs because of sex. Do you want sex badly enough to lose your job, or get extorted by a spurned lover who is threatening you? If not, then it is best to keep your pants on and pass on that offer of free sex. Nothing is ever free.

Staying Safe

> *"'Just saying no' prevents teenage pregnancy the way*
> *'Have a nice day' cures chronic depression."*
> *- Faye Wattleton*

Because the diseases you can catch via sex can kill you, it is extremely important that you protect yourself. Getting pregnant may be the least of your worries. In order to stay safe, you need to use protection, and the cheapest and most effective form of protection against both pregnancies and STDs is a condom.

In this day and age if you are living in America there are no longer any excuses not to practice safe sex. Condoms are readily available and you don't need to talk to anyone to get one. All you have to do is pick them out at your local supermarket or drugstore and pay for them. Don't feel embarrassed about the checkout person noticing them. Purchasing a condom means you are a responsible adult and that is something to be proud of. If you are too embarrassed to purchase a condom let along talk about condom use with your partner, then you are too young and immature to be having sex.

When used properly, latex condoms are over 99 percent effective at preventing pregnancies. And because latex is an impenetrable barrier to viruses, including the AIDS virus they are also 99 percent effective at preventing STDs. Natural-membrane condoms are only slightly less effective because of the natural pores in the membrane, but if you are allergic to latex, by all means, use a natural-membrane condom, as they are way more effective than no protection at all.

In order for a condom to be effective, you need to use them properly, that means three things:

1) Check the condom for tears (old condoms tend to disintegrate and it is recommended that you not use a condom over 6 months old);
2) Put it on properly (if you aren't sure, find out); and
3) Use it every time. That means use condoms for oral and anal sex in addition to vaginal sex. (If you are engaging in oral sex, it should go without saying that you should not use a condom with spermicidal jelly).

Other Things You Should Know

There are a wide range of condom styles and brands available in the United States. Some of them are excellent when it comes to mutual satisfaction. What this means is that men can no longer use the excuse that they can't feel anything as a way to avoid using a condom. Try several out and you will eventually find one that is perfect for you and that might actually increase your pleasure. So there really are no excuses.

Any guy trying to weasel out of using a condom should be viewed as a health risk and you should not have sex with him. Consider this: if they don't want to use a condom with you, then chances are they have had unprotected sex with their other partners and if you engage with them, you will be picking up whatever diseases the people in this guys love chain have. Best to avoid this sort of idiot.

Testing for STDs

If you are in a relationship and are getting ready to take it to the next level, then you should both get tested for STDs. After all, if you love this person, you will not want to put their health at risk because you didn't know you had a transmittable disease. Getting tested helps you both to be safe and that is what it means to be responsible. And again, if you aren't comfortable discussing this with your partner, you probably shouldn't be having sex. Responsible adults don't think twice about discussing these important matters before becoming more intimate.

AIDS tests and tests for other STDs are readily available at your local health clinic, and if you are sexually active, it is a good idea to get tested for HIV every 6 months. Consider it part of being a responsible adult. After all, this is just about you being responsible. The problem is that you can never really know what the sexual background of your partner really is. Some people are unfaithful and irresponsible when it comes to relationships and sex, and these are they very same people who will lie to you about their past. While you obviously want to have faith that your partner is being honest with you, it is always good idea to verify both your and their health statuses anyway. As unfortunate as it is, infidelity happens.

If your partner doesn't want to get tested, this should send up red flags. Someone who doesn't want to get tested for STDs is most likely worried that they have something. The most likely reason for someone having an STD is that they have had lots of partners and didn't always use protection. Regardless, if someone doesn't want to get tested, they should be considered high risk. To be safe and because you can never really be sure whether what you have been told is really true, get tested regularly.

Pornography

> *"The line between protected pornography and unprotected obscenity lies between appealing to a good healthy interest in sex and appealing to a depraved interest, whatever that means."*
>
> *- Antonin Scalia*

While there is nothing wrong with indulging in pornography, you really need to keep in mind that it isn't real. In the real world people aren't actually able to have sex for four straight hours, not without chemical assistance anyway, and even with chemical assistance, a four-hour plus hard-on is cause for medical intervention. Farm girls are rarely scantily dressed and they and their twin are rarely waiting for a guy to come along so they can have sex in the hayloft with him. Pornography is just another form of fantasy.

The biggest problem people run into when consuming pornography is that they lose their sense of reality. If you are expecting from life what you fantasize about through pornography, you will be a very disappointed person indeed. Keep in mind that a lot of the things depicted, especially in the erotic literature, aren't physically possible. If you are trying to live up to an impossible ideal, you will always fall short, and as a result will never be happy.

Another problem with pornography is that it can be addictive. If it takes you away from dealing productively with the world as it is, and not as you fantasize it to be, it will cause problems. Some people with addictive personalities get lost in the pornographic fantasy and never re-emerge. That is bad, and doesn't lead to happiness.

Finally, on the subject of violent porn: when you combine addictive personalities and a basic inability to discern between fantasy and reality with violent forms of pornography, the result is an increase in bizarre violent crimes.

This has probably always been a problem, but, with the easy availability of cheap or free porn, including the really violent sort that is now available on the internet, porn transforms from a harmless (lets look at the latest issue of Playboy behind the bleachers activity) into a catalyst for some really violent crimes perpetrated by sick individuals who want to act out what they are fantasizing. And, since what they are fantasizing about has grown increasingly bizarre as their access to a wide range of really sick pornography has grown, we are now seeing some previously unthinkable crimes occurring on a more frequent basis. Don't let this happen to you. Keep your perspective and remember that fairy tales are fine and dandy, but real life is what you really fancy.

The Humanist Approach to Sex

> *"In all sexual encounters, commitment to humane and humanistic values should be present."*
> - *The American Humanist Association, Sexual Bill of Rights and Responsibilities*

Sex is a big deal. There are consequences to having sex and you should be prepared for those consequences before engaging in sex with anyone. The Humanist approach to sexuality is that it should be pleasurable, loving, and free of guilt. But that doesn't mean that anything goes. With the freedom to express your sexuality comes responsibility. From a Humanist perspective, sexual morality cannot be separated from general morality. Both must include compassion, ethics, and responsibility.

Whether any given sex act is morally acceptable from a Humanist perspective really depends on whether it helps the people involved become happy or causes suffering. Sexual pleasure must not come at the expense of someone else's happiness.

To make sure sex is a source of both pleasure and happiness for you, take precautions to keep yourself and your partners safe. Don't develop unrealistic expectations for yourself or your partners through the irresponsible use of pornography or other forms of sexually fantasy. Choose your partners wisely. And always approach sex as a responsible, educated, compassionate, and ethical person.

Help—I Think I'm Dying!

"There were many ways of breaking a heart. Stories were full of hearts broken by love, but what really broke a heart was taking away its dream—whatever that dream might be."

- Pearl S Buck

As with all aspects of life, Humanists approach grief rationally and compassionately. At some point in your life, you will experience grief to a greater or lesser extent. Someone you care about may die, sometimes unexpectedly. You will most likely have your heart broken. Or you may experience some sort of physical trauma. These are all things we know that if we experience them, will cause us to grieve.

There is very little written on the subject of Humanist grief, but what I can tell you is that the Humanist inclination is to approach grief with an eye on the future. Our goal is to survive grief and go on to live a happy and productive life despite our grief. I have spoken to a lot of Humanists on the subject of grief and have been given advice by them to help with my own grieving process when my daughter died, and this really does seem to be the general Humanist approach.

Along these lines, when we Humanists grieve, we try to focus our attention on the fact that our grief is directly related to our happiness. You can see this reflected in Humanist memorial services, where we focus on the life of the deceased and the joy and happiness that individual brought to our lives as a way to deal with our grief.

A basic rule of thumb is that the amount of grief you experience is inversely proportional to the amount of joy whatever you are grieving gave you. In other words, if something gave you a tremendous amount of joy, losing it will cause you a tremendous amount of emotional grief. This is why losing a child is one of the most painful experiences anyone can go through. So painful that many marriages don't survive the loss of a child.

Don't Get Me Wrong

> *"The deep pain that is felt at the death of every friendly*
> *soul arises from the feeling that there is in every individual*
> *something which is inexpressible, peculiar to him alone,*
> *and is, therefore, absolutely and irretrievably lost."*
> — Arthur Schopenhauer

Grief is a painful experience, both emotionally and physically, hence the title of this chapter. If you have experienced grief, you will know that you sometimes think you are dying because of it. If the grief is great enough, death might seem like a relief.

Most people might be surprised, though, to realize that grief can also occur for much more benign reasons. The quote at the beginning of this chapter is true. What breaks a heart is taking away its dream. People often grieve changes in lifestyle, even if they wanted to make the change. Changes in jobs, even if good, mean you are leaving a job you might have liked and that all the possibilities of that old job and friendships are now gone. I have grieved to a greater or lesser extent every time I have moved to a new place.

Obviously, when the grief is minimal, it is fairly easy to get through the experience. However, when the grief is great, there are three basic rules to remember to get through the experience without adding additional trauma to an already painful experience: let it flow, let it go, and choose your memories wisely.

Let It Flow

> *"It is some relief to weep; grief is satisfied and carried off*
> *by tears. "*
> — Ovid

The first thing to remember is that grief is an emotion. And, like all emotions, it comes and goes and comes again. Hence, the metaphor, *waves of emotion*. The great thing about emotions, including the painful ones, is that they are temporary. Grief works like any of your other emotions. Once you experience it, your mind will eventually move on to other things and other emotions. So, allow your mind to grieve and let your emotions flow naturally without intellectual interference.

Don't be afraid to experience your emotions. Yes, grief can be incredibly painful. But trying to not experience it won't work. The only thing you will accomplish by trying not to experience the pain of grief is the prolonging of your grief, and why would anyone want to do that? The main problem with trying to avoid grief is that you are always aware of its presence. While you are trying to avoid it you are still experiencing low levels of it. The smarter way to deal with it is to simply experience the waves of grief as they come. I have always found that waves of emotion are actually easier to bear because at least with waves there are breaks from the emotion.

Her Tears Flowed Like Wine

If you need to cry, it is best to let the tears flow. Don't deny yourself this therapeutic urge. If you are grieving something, it is perfectly normal and acceptable to cry. Crying helps purge your body of an overwhelming emotion. You hold tears back at your own risk.

If you need to cry and attempt to stem that tide you will only cause yourself additional grief. Obviously, there are more appropriate times than others to do your crying, but if you feel the need, indulge yourself. You will feel better, even if you are a little embarrassed afterward. Crying will definitely relieve some of your stress.

For major things, such as the death of a child, don't be surprised if you burst out in tears in the supermarket checkout line. You don't have to be strong or hold it in. If anyone has earned the right to cry, it is you.

However, if you are grieving a change in job, you might want to try and schedule your crying time to when you are alone in your own home when no one is watching. Consider it a guilty pleasure.

The other important thing to know about crying is that it is physically impossible to cry for very long. Like all emotions, it will come and go. You will eventually stop, even if it is just to fall asleep from exhaustion.

My Advice

Cry if you need to. Don't be embarrassed by it. You have earned the right to cry. But if you are grieving anything less than the death of a loved one, try not to impose your tears on others. In most cases, you should probably try to do your crying in private. The exception is of course when you are offered a shoulder to cry on. Then feel free to go ahead and get your tears and snot on the offered shoulder.

Let It Go

> *"When you are sorrowful look again in your heart, and you shall see that in truth you are weeping for that which has been your delight."*
>
> *- Kahlil Gibran*

If you have experienced something that has caused you to grieve, then you, above all others, have earned a little happiness. Don't deny yourself little rays of happiness in the otherwise turbulent storm of grief.

It is amazing to me how many people hold onto their grief. They don't want to let it flow and let it go for even a few moments. It's as if they think that allowing their emotions to ebb and flow is somehow a betrayal to the depth of feeling they held for what they are grieving. Don't fall into this trap. Grief is an emotion and there is no wrong or right way to experience it. If you smile at a joke or at the sight of a flower, or laugh at how wet your pillow is after a crying jag, it doesn't mean that your emotions weren't real or strong or that you didn't care. It only means that you are allowing your emotions to flow normally without intellectual interference. It means you are an emotionally healthy individual.

Being emotionally healthy and allowing your emotions to ebb and flow is a good thing. People who practically force their grief onto themselves aren't emotionally healthy. Just as trying to keep grief away doesn't work and is actually counter productive, trying to keep grief front and center doesn't work either. Your brain won't let you. If you try, you will end up beating yourself up for failure and that will only make you feel worse, not better. The whole point of grief is to eventually feel better.

Time Heals All Wounds

This normal ebb and low of grief is why the phrase "time heals all wounds" resonates so well. It isn't that your grief magically disappears at some point in time; it is rather that if you allow your emotions to ebb and flow, eventually you will feel less grief and more happiness. If you try to force your emotions to stay at bay or stay in your face, you are not allowing your natural emotional ebb and flow to occur and aren't, as they say, letting go.

If you are having trouble allowing yourself small moments of happiness then consider this: after all you have been through, haven't you earned a little happiness? Don't deny yourself these small moments of happiness. They are precious and you shouldn't waste them by reprimanding yourself for experiencing them.

My Advice

Emotions are temporary things. They ebb and flow, and it is usually best to allow them to ebb and flow rather than trying to force them into a pattern you think is right. Don't worry about moments of happiness in a sea of grief. If your grief is severe, your grief will return, have no doubt about that. View these small respites as something to be welcomed and eventually you will experience them more frequently and for longer periods of time.

Other Baggage

> "Anger is never without a reason, but seldom with a good one."
>
> - Benjamin Franklin

Grief and sadness aren't the only emotions you will feel during a period of grief. There are a lot of ancillary emotions that come with grief, especially anger and depression. Realize that these are natural emotions to feel and you should allow yourself to experience them. It is important, however, to not get stuck on these emotions. They should ebb and flow as your other emotions do.

The problem is that people often get wrapped up in their grief-related emotions, they attach more importance to them than is normally warranted. When grieving, we all have a tendency to try and make our anger and/or depression the primary emotions we feel. This is understandable because as bad as anger and depression are to experience, they are exponentially less painful than grief. The point you need to remember is to not hold onto your grief-related anger or depression. Let it go and let it flow as you do your other emotions.

Anger

This is especially important with grief-related anger because this sort of anger is often displaced. It is an especially bad idea to actually act on displaced anger. Allow your grief-related anger to ebb and flow and see if it sticks around after the lion's share of the grief has gone away before taking your grief-related anger seriously. The other benefit of allowing your anger to ebb and flow is that once it has ebbed, you will have more perspective on it. Given enough time you may discover that your anger was silly and misplaced.

For Example

When grieving the loss of my daughter, I actually had a lot of anger towards, of all people, a now-famous movie director. It's kind of a long story going back to when I was in high school. The point is he had nothing to do with the death of my daughter. My anger with him was totally misplaced. It was pretty silly really.

A Word About Faith

Faith can be a very contentious thing during periods of grief. I have no doubt that many people find solace in their faith, but for many people faith is a source of anger and conflict during periods of grief.

For those of you, to whom faith is a source of comfort, please be aware that this isn't the case for everyone. Don't assume that what works for you will work for others. And, if you are a person of faith and find yourself becoming angry with God, go back and reread my section about displaced anger.

My Advice

It goes without saying that not acting on grief-related anger is super-doubly important if you are grieving a broken heart. Don't act on your anger until you are over your grief. Just don't. Let it go and congratulate yourself on how mature you are being despite your overwhelming urges to seek revenge. Keep reminding yourself that you are an ethical, compassionate, and responsible person and that you aren't the sort to do something irrational or stupid.

Memories

> "That which is dreamed can never be lost, can never be undreamed."
>
> - Master Li (in Neil Gaiman's Sandman comic)

It is wrong to think that you will or should get over your grief. It is more accurate to say that you will eventually learn to live with the loss. If you allow yourself to grieve and allow your emotions to ebb and flow, you will eventually integrate that loss into your life and while it may still be sad, it won't be quite as painful. Eventually you will be able to get on with your life and be able to do everyday things such as shopping without bursting out crying at the sappy song playing on the radio.

The best way to integrate a loss into your life is to seek out happy memories. Your memories of whatever it is you lost will be what remain, and you need to find a place for them. Try to make the memories you focus on happy ones. That way, when you do find yourself reminiscing, it will bring you a melancholy joy and not as much pain and sadness.

While this last bit of advice is good, it is only partially applicable to the grief of a broken heart. Too many happy thoughts about a relationship that ended might encourage you to seek your ex out, and that is a bad idea. You are no longer together for a reason. What is broken up should stay broken up. On the other hand, if ten years after you had your heart broken, you are still getting angry and sad and upset when you think of your ex, you need to try something else, and I would suggest that something else should be professional counseling.

The Humanist Approach to Grief

"If you're going through hell, keep going."
- Winston Churchill

While grief is indeed painful, Humanists view it as a normal part of life. It is not something you should run from, but neither should you suffer from it unnecessarily. The goal of the Humanist is to be happy and so we approach our grief rationally and compassionately. We allow ourselves to grieve and to find happiness in our grief and eventually let go of the grief so that we can live fully in our futures.

Grief is painful, but it is an emotion and emotions ebb and flow. Allow yourself to grieve, but don't hold onto your grief either. Allow yourself to find moments of happiness and eventually you will feel less pain and more happiness.

After the death of my daughter, I joined a few grief support groups specifically for people who had lost children. I wasn't too surprised to find that most people put too much pressure on themselves during times of grief. Most were concerned about their level of grief. Were they grieving too much? Not enough? Don't worry about those things. Everyone grieves differently. How you grieve is right for you. Do some research and learn what the experts on grief have to say. Most of all, be prepared for your emotions to be all over the place and be compassionate with yourself.

The thing that really amazed me though as I participated in these grieving groups, was how many people refused to be happy or to seek happiness after the loss of a loved one. It was like they felt that being happy was somehow a betrayal of the person they had lost. That concept is really lost on a Humanist. Perhaps it is our rationality that helps us through. But as far as I am concerned, if there is such a thing as sin, suffering must be a sin. Sometimes you can't avoid suffering. But it seems to me it would be better to be happy. If you are planning to continue living despite your loss, it would probably be a good idea to at least try to get on with being happy.

I guess when it comes to grief; this simple inescapable truth is what motivates a Humanist in our times of grief: since we plan to go on living because we like being alive, we might as well be happy. We have nothing to be ashamed of in taking this approach. It is rational, compassionate, and responsible. We don't hide from the pain of grief, instead choosing to view it as a reflection of the joy and love we feel from what we lost.

Conclusion

"Happiness is the only good. The place to be happy is here. The time to be happy is now. The way to be happy is to help make others so."

-   Robert Ingersoll

The Humanist approach to happiness is simple. Be a good person. Strive to be ethical, compassionate and responsible in all that you do. Take responsibility for your life and for the consequences of your actions. Choose to act in ways that will increase your happiness and the happiness of others.

Remember that happiness and pleasure are not the same thing and that sometimes the pursuit of pleasure can actually make you less happy. When choosing between pleasure and happiness, choose happiness.

Because happiness is so dependent on the outcomes of your actions, remember to engage in reality-based decision making and problem solving. The more you understand the true nature of your problems, the more effective your solutions will be. The more effective you are, the better your outcomes will be. The better your outcomes are, the happier you are likely to be.

And finally, happiness isn't a result of what you accomplish. There are plenty of people who are very successful in their working lives, but who are miserable as individuals. Being happy requires you to be happy with who you are as a person. And that brings us back to the beginning. If you want to be happy, be a good person and help others to be happy too.

About the Author:

Jennifer Hancock is a writer, speaker and Humanist. She can be found on the web at www.Jen-Hancock.com

6657188R0

Made in the USA
Charleston, SC
19 November 2010